NEW WINE PUBLISHING

P. O. Box 5113, Edmeston, NY 13335, USA.
www.newwinepublishing.com

The Love Essence
Love Divine

Copyright © All rights reserved author Dr. Joseph Luxum

ISBN-13: 9781937635176
ISBN-10: 1937635171

No part of this book may be reproduced, stored in a retrieval system, or transmitted by any means without the written permission of the author.

Unless specified otherwise all Bible quotations are from the New American Standard Bible Translation.

Printed in the United States of America.

Table of Contents

The healing essence of love 3
Being His Mouth 4
Understanding the love essence 12
Why praying for our enemy? 15
The nine fruits 25
Holy, set apart, exclusive 27
Drawing the love essence 31
The God essence 37
God's tender mercies 39
The last is first and the first is last 44
God's plans for you 48
God's love expressed through a ministry 49
Called out of Darkness 55
Born of love 57
Endless Love 69
God's love for His chosen 73
God's love & hell 83
God's love & Satan 88
The heavenly love & peace 93
When I repented 101

THE LOVE ESSENCE
The flow of God's love in your life

Chapter 1

THE HEALING ESSENCE OF LOVE

Jesus spoke of the love essence in this sentence (John 17:26) 'the love with which You loved Me.'

This is intriguing, for He spoke of love as of a resident and a residence-changing substance, or even of a river that flows from one into another. What kind of love was He speaking about; and how can we get it? But can we get it to keep it? Is it obtainable, or it comes when it is given?

These questions may lead to discovery. In my spirit-man I sense that I am opening myself to something new and profoundly involving and glorious at the same time.

Just recently, I had an experience with God, at night, where He challenged me to spiritually travel to anyone I was hurt by. I traveled, touching my cheek to my enemy's cheek forgiving him or her, telling them, 'I love you no matter what.' When I returned from the seemingly all-night journey, I was spiritually high. No drug could ever induce such euphoria. I turned over and with a smiling grin on my face fell into deep sleep. The night seemed endless and my exploration of God's love had just begun. I hope that you could experience it too. And that's the reason why I need to tell you about it and lead you along the path, which will point you in that direction. Since I cannot make you do anything you don't want to, but perhaps wish to, I can only show you the reasons why the essence of God's love really works when one wants to be completely healed and move forward on the path of righteousness, perfection and utter happiness.

Let me start with the fact that the Bible mentions something about God being with one's mouth and in this case with my mind, thoughts and actions.

[Exodus 4:15] I will be with your mouth and his mouth, and I will teach you what you are to do.

Therefore I yield my entire being to the Lord's wisdom and bathe in His grace. Let Him speak now and teach us His ways.

***

Chapter 2

BEING HIS MOUTH

God spoke through His prophet [Jeremiah 15:19] saying: "If you extract the precious from the worthless, you will become My spokesman." The original Hebrew does not read as 'spokesman,' but exactly MOUTH. God's mouth; or as God's mouth. So let's reread this verse again: "If you extract the precious from the worthless, you will become as My mouth."

Before we step on the core theme, the LOVE ESSENCE, we must detach ourselves from ourselves and get attached to God who is called the PERFECT LOVE. That love casts out, or dispels ALL FEAR.

Lovely. Now, let's create timidity or a fear-free environment, an atmosphere in which the love essence can manifest itself. In His priestly prayer Jesus said,

[John 17:26] I have made Your name known to them, and will make it known, so that the love with which You loved Me may be in them, and I in them.

He speaks of God's name in connection with love, which the Father and Son share. Sharing is the word. A self-love is no love at all for love is like a living, vibrant and moving essence to be exchanged between at least two beings, spiritual or natural.

In Islam, God is not called the Father. Islam makes no provision for its faithful adherents to even entertain the loving idea of God being a Father and therefore having children. As it is widely believed in Christianity Islam teaches that God does not have a son. In my view, it is dictatorial and consequently enslaving.

Love, as the spiritual essence, which cannot ever exist in a dictatorial environment. Dictatorship turns into oppression and oppression thrusts love out from its presence. Just as the oppression presence is nasty and unpleasant, to say the least, the love presence is pleasant. It brings you the true state of happiness. Many seek happiness, but do not know how to obtain it. Just as there are laws governing gravity so there are laws governing the exchange and presence of love.

God always showed love through deliverance and liberation. As we read the history of Israel we find numerous accounts of His people crying to God. God responded by raising liberators, beginning with Moses who was sent to Egypt to liberate his people; Samson; Gideon; and finally Jesus. *To liberate the oppressed, to open prison doors and set the captives free*; Jesus declared quoting Isaiah 61:1-3.

God gave us the opportunity to eat of the tree of knowledge of the plus and of the minus and with that contrast the aim was to bring us to the point of decision and choice. We choose Him by loving Him; as a result we would also love one another. Love without choice is powerless. One might as well enslave love and use it like those ladies in a harem.

God wanted to be loved by choice. That's why He sent a beast of the field called Nechash (an angel we today call Satan). Through this legibly speaking animal God created a new desire for no other tree but the Tree of Knowledge.

As it is later portrayed a donkey also spoke with human voice because God spoke through His angel who spoke through that animal (Numbers 22:28).

The picture of trees speaks of contrasts, with which both; the awareness and perception would then be activated. After contrasts were created/activated Eve and Adam were able to choose.

Next to that tree of knowledge/awareness stood the Tree of Life. But before the appearance of Nechash for neither tree Eve had any desire. That desire was either freshly created or was awakened out of slumber.

Contrasts create the power to choose and with it a resolve. Between red and blue I chose one or the other color. With that same power Enoch chose to walk with God and was no more for God took him alive; this kind of immortality God planned for us all.

[Deuteronomy 30:19] I have set before you life and death, the blessing and the curse. So choose life in order that you may live.

God wants to be chosen like a lady awaits her beloved to choose her for his wife. Without contrasting possibilities love ceases all activities and its essence does not flow from one heart into another. God wanted to be loved. Awesome!

In Judaism no observant Jew can call God as 'my' Father. However, God can be called as AVEENU, our Father. The sense of His fatherhood is rooted in Him being our Creator and therefore the Father of all things.

Only in Christianity we find something totally new; an introduction to God as the Heavenly Father Jesus taught us to pray, "Our Father who art in heaven."

I do not know about you, but I am drawn to something lovely and loving. I find in my emotional and spiritual makeup the need to be loved and to give love.

The loving process begins already in the mother's womb. The entire fetus formation process is laden with love.

Love is the root and its offshoots are: compassion, mercy, gentleness, care, thoughtfulness and loving-kindness.

The word "compassion" (Hebrew RAHAMEEM) means exactly tender mercies in plural, and its root is REHAM, which means womb. Just as in the mother's womb there are protective walls surrounding the fetus, so it is with God's tender mercies, which are endless.

King David spoke much about God's mercies. God is love having no beginning and no end. Only anything physical has a beginning and an end; anything spiritual is timeless and therefore endless.

God is Spirit therefore He has no silhouette, nothing physically seen, which then could be painted or sculptured. God, portrayed as love, is only found in the New Testament's gospels and the letters of John the beloved. And speaking of the BE-Loved, we find a similarity in the choice of names in the Old Testament, where God had called someone Jedidiah (YEDIDYAH the Lord's beloved). That someone was King Solomon. Imagine. Because of David's adulterous sin with Bathsheba, which led to a quite deliberate and despicable act of her husband's murder, Uriah, their first child died. The second child was Solomon. David sinned with Bathsheba and she was as guilty as David.

David repented. He cried to God and was truly sorry, taking all the punishments he could endure, and that touched God's heart. To God flesh itself has but a little meaning, yet it is precious because of its spiritual cargo. The first child, as it were, experienced God's severe wrath and again, as it were, that wrath atoned for David's sin. But the second child experienced grace. God's love always prevails. When God relents, then in that act, grace is born and then abundant love begins to flow again. Once you know God's nature it becomes easier to bathe in His love. So learn about these mechanisms.

If we look a bit further back, we also see that Cain was wrathful, while Abel peaceable. The reason why Cain was wrathful is perhaps that he opened Eve's womb. She bore for the very first time and was experiencing childbirth pains; and when that curse expressed itself she most certainly hated it and plausibly even her firstborn. Ever since Cain God seeks the firstborns.

Remember the fact that with the curse and in its consequences God provided repentance. True repentance erases curses. I know this for I have repented myself with deep sorrow (in the last chapter I share this in more detail.)

I also prayed for pregnant ladies and ladies without ovaries. Here are four examples.

In the early 90's I ministered in a church of the late pastor Polizzi in Troy, Illinois. Directly from a clink comes a young lady. "My baby is dead." She weeps saying, "I must be operated." And then she looks at me with anticipation. I was a complete stranger to her. (But God loves pregnant mothers, even if they have conceived after being raped or have fornicated). God's mercy for new life is enormous. In the name of Jesus I have removed death from her womb. I touched her belly and spoke to the dead child to come alive.

A year later I happened to minister in the same church again. Beaming-faced young lady comes to me carrying a baby. She said this baby was once dead, but now is alive. With tears of joy streaming down her face she told me about her experience. When I called for life she felt her baby kick. She went to the clinic. But this time, low and behold the baby was alive and healthy and not brain damaged. In God time does not exist.

The second lady had no ovaries but only a desire to be a mother; she was operated and both of her ovaries have been removed. She had no uterus anymore. I asked her if she has that intense desire to become a mother. She said that it is overwhelmingly so. "In that case, I see that it was God who planed this desire in you," I said. I laid hands on her prophesying supernatural pregnancy and birth.

Next year in the same place there comes the smiling lady with a baby stroller. Without hesitation she said to all present how the man of God prophesied over her and she supernaturally conceived and bore a child. She took her baby out of the stroller and showed it to all.

The third lady already had 7 children and was pregnant with her eighth. She told me that each time the birth is long and very painful and now she is afraid of going through it again. It happens that I preached about repentance and that Jesus atoned for all curses. I then laid hands on her and told her that this birth will be different, quick and painless. Come next year and she gives birth to a baby boy. The birth was under three minutes and without pain. Out of gratitude she named her boy after me.

The fourth pregnant young lady was in Rotterdam, Netherlands while I was in New York. I was called to pray for her. The umbilical cord was wrapped around the baby's neck asphyxiating it. The doctor decided to operate soon after the baby dies. That was not a pretty picture. The heartbeat was faint. On the phone I said to the lady that at this very moment her baby is turning by itself in her belly. At that moment the baby turned. She excitedly confirmed that at that precise moment the baby was energized and she felt it turning into the right position getting ready to be born.

The baby untangled itself.

I told her to go to the doctor and be examined again. Lo and behold the baby's umbilical cord was untied and the heart rate became normal. On December 17th 2012 the mother gave birth to a healthy baby. For more examples of God's awesome love visit our website, luxumlight.com/miracles).

There are many more miracles than we have recorded; they are happening today because of God's love and not some magical faith.

Have faith in God's love and His unending mercies. Nonetheless, the precondition is your love for your Father; and if so, then you will study Him and His ways.

Once this becomes part of your life; something new will happen in both your brain as well your mind.

Some suggest that Cain and Abel were twins because of the Hebrew word 'continued' or 'again'. Also, the words 'conceived again' are missing when the birth of Abel was mentioned, which might suggest that Eve continued giving birth while still in the same labor. Whether they were twins or not, Cain opened Eve's womb in pain and hence he was associated with the curse. Abel's birth was perhaps easier. And when Cain observed this contrast and the preferential treatment of his brother, not only by their parents but above all by God, Cain vented his resentment against his brother.

Today, we read in the New Testament about the nine fruits and the nine gifts of the Holy Spirit, but only the nine fruits begin with the greatest fruit of them all, love. By bearing these nine fruits, one overcomes the obstacles life presents us with.

God spoke to Cain about this mastering, subduing, ruling over, and overcoming (Genesis 4:7), but instead of being willing to do that he slew his own brother. Cain had a choice, for his parents already then tasted of the Tree of Knowledge; they knew the difference, simply by seeing that knowledge's consequences, which weren't too pleasant.

After these unpleasant experiences they were given another power, which was the powerful agency of choice. Love is not a program that the human robot automatically responds to. We can choose, accept or reject; we choose to love our Maker by studying Him and His ways, or by being stuck in the self-love. However, religion has never provided such answers because religion is stuck in the 'original sin', which supposedly Adam and Eve gave us. Religion dooms us to death and instead of giving us intelligence it controls us with foolishness. Jesus came to free us from it; and in which freedom we can choose to study God in truth and on our own. All I do is only point you in the right direction. The rest is up to you.

We need no organization between God and man, no philosophy; and most certainly no theology. We need no opposing camps of creed or disagreements. We need freedom.

So choose life... But choose how? The sentence ends with, by loving the LORD.

All one needs to do is repent, humble the pride of life with which every human being is born, and that's what David did. King David knew God's ways, and how to reach Him.

[Numbers 14:18] The LORD is slow to anger and abundant in lovingkindness, forgiving iniquity and transgression; but He will by no means clear the guilty, visiting the iniquity of the fathers on the children to the third and the fourth generations.'

Yes, there are special mechanisms that touch and extract God's forgiving tender love. However, the responsibility to humble this earth and flesh born pride lies in our willingness—in the name of love for Him—to bring it down at God's footstool. Only in connection with God are we requested to humble the pride of life and walk humbly with Him, never with people, especially with strangers. As long as the pride of life rules your behavior and attitude—when approaching or dealing with God and His realm—you would never be able to walk with God at all. Enoch WALKED with God and God took Him—Genesis 5:24 informs us. This walking with your Maker is nothing else than humbling of the pride of this earthly life and getting filled with His love to overflowing. This overflow had to be indeed great for in the midst of perversions and severe lawlessness only one had pleased the Creator—Enoch.

[Micah 6:8] He has told you, O man, what is good; and what does the LORD require of you, but to do justice, to love kindness, and to walk humbly with your God?

The humbling of pride before the Lord is nothing else than making room for His presence. In other words, the willing decision to prepare Him a room and allowing His love to flow into one's life like the healing Balm of Gilead. It's an act of invitation. It is required that one becomes a vessel of honor, empty of self and ego; otherwise no healing can take place.

Do we need healing, but perhaps not in the sense that we understand healing? Nonetheless, everyone needs healing because we are not well until we find ourselves bathing in His love's essence; then, when we look back, we realize that we were not well at all. Love, as all rivers, also needs a riverbed. But no river climbs, but seeks lower and softer places to carve out its bed. After we strip off any sophistication and acquired illusions, which we have treated as something we must have for the society dictates it so, we allow ourselves to become like little children, honest and truthful. The same is true with the essence of His love.

*   *   *

Chapter 3

UNDERSTANDING THE LOVE ESSENCE

There is not even one place in the Bible that mentions angels as being created according to God's image and likeness. That's because angels are flames, winds and ministering spirits solely dependent on God. They have no free will simply because they have no pride, and they have no pride because they do not have physical bodies as we do.

Between God and earthlings are the angels who are like beacons of light, messengers, serving as conduits between God and us. Angels don't teach, instruct or preach; that task belongs us. If they ask questions then they do not do that from their own selves, but God asks those questions through them.

If God reasons with us, He does so through one of His spirits, winds, and flames. Just as an ambassador does not speak from him or herself but from the top and unified headship of a government.

[Job 40:7] Now gird up your loins like a man; I will ask you, and you instruct Me.

[Isaiah 1:18] "Come now, and let us reason together," says the LORD.

Sooner or later you will realize that God does not reason with you using isolated verses dealing with pieces, but the ONE God. His logic is one and all fragments of information point to the One and His oneness.

Once you recognize this unity, you will stop arguing in the natural and very human pompous pride, and like Job (42:6) you will say, "Therefore I retract, and I repent in dust and ashes." And that is the state of being when one starts to absorb the heavenly logic like a sponge; and then all scriptures begin to flow together in perfect harmony.

In heaven God's love permeates all spiritual beings and that is the reason why there is no need for hierarchy. God the Perfect Love dispels all fear in an instant. Naturally, all are subject to God and are only prompted by the impulse of love.

It was love that motivated God to make us; and only we have the will and freedom to go astray, disobey, to reason and use logic; angels do not. Angels, being the extensions of God's love, are there to serve us. That's how important we are to God.

We can serve God or we don't have to, we can obey Him or disobey Him, but the moment we completely subject ourselves to Him that act becomes most precious to God for then we become like angels.

This complete subordination is motivated by love; never fear, which involves threats of hell's fire and brimstone. Once we permit this love essence to saturate our lives we begin to blend with our Maker until we become indeed one with Him.

Poetically spoken, angels are eager to look into these things.

[1 Peter 1:12] It was revealed to them that they were not serving themselves, but you, in these things which now have been announced to you through those who preached the gospel to you by the Holy Spirit sent from heaven—things into which angels long to look.

In fact, angels are neither eager nor long for anything. They do not experience the same contrasts as we do; like cold and heat, illness or health, hunger or thirst, night or day. They do not find any opposition in heaven. They enjoy perfect peace. Even the word 'enjoy' does not apply for in order to enjoy something its opposites must be present.

Jesus said that only in this world we have tribulation, but in Him we have peace and that peace is confidence and complete security (John 14:27). Yes, security is peace. Insecurity brings unrest. The heavenly peace brings the complete security.

[John 16:33] These things I have spoken to you, so that in Me you may have peace. In the world you have tribulation, but take courage; I have overcome the world.

Heaven experiences no tribulation. If it did, then it would not be heaven, but something we know nothing about and definitely would not want to spend eternity in. Either heaven is completely secure and peaceful or it is a sucked out of a thumb mystical sphere. However, a group of people no longer speculates but knows. The seed of wrath and violence blinds, but the seed of peace opens up.

The peacemakers are blessed for they are called sons of God (Matthew 5:9); so heaven must be filled not with warmakers, but peacemakers. God would not be the Perfect Love, which casts out *all* fear (from its presence) by mixing the temporary (physical earth) with the spiritual. He does not seek soldiers but sons. It would be hard to have a loving fellowship with warriors and killers.

[Matthew 5:44-45] Jesus said: love your enemies and pray for those who persecute you, **so that you may be sons of your Father who is in heaven.**

We create peace out of love, just as wars originate in the pride of this physical life, which by then is already charged with hate. Those emotions cannot be rationalized. Hate is an unstable emotion. Haters need healing and that healing can only happen through love. To love your enemy means to heal anyone that made him or herself into your enemy.

* * *

Chapter 1

WHY PRAYING FOR OUR ENEMY?

God is love. Period. His essence is love, in which one will never find any double talk, ulterior motives; like seizing an advantageous occasion because someone has made him or herself vulnerable. I have no enemies that I know of. As a standard of God's love I am consciously or subconsciously and continually involved in healing. In my presence enmity melts. However, usually those that set themselves as my enemy avoid any contact with me; for once they connect, then God's love like electricity travels to them and they can't stand it. Either they run away or sink deeper into the state of envious melancholy.

People are emotionally mixed up. They do not know what they feel and why the feel animosity, love or hatred. These sentiments are often being manipulated with definitions of patriotism, allegiance, camaraderie, loyalty... etc. Many people believed in the world-improving mission of Napoleon. They died for him and for his vision because they believed in him. What a waste. Many have been duped into believing in an ideal because they do not believe in the God-sent truth. Conclusively, man's convincing and appealing truth fills the void. On one hand human (religious and Kenite) forces deprive you of the truth that would liberate you from all falsehood, and on the other hand—for lack of alternatives—you do not have the freedom to choose. We are told to use sympathy for some, but vent enmity towards others in the name of... whatever.

The potency of divine love is immeasurable and it can be experienced. I am experiencing it; sometimes so strong that I feel that I can float. If I did not experience it first, after granting God my permission to overpower me with His love, I would only blabber and ramble, using, void of any practical basis catchy and good sounding sentences.

Am I trying to overpower you? - Absolutely! Yes, I am trying to conquer you with God's love just as I have been conquered. The ball is now in your court.

In order to experience that awesome power and have the essence of His love to flow into one's life one must give God permission; an unrestricted and unconditional access.

Understanding, accepting and then acting upon that which is being said here, will eventually bring that wonderful experience. Trust me. I know what I'm talking about. You just have to trust me. I write it for you because I act on His love poured out for you my dear friend.

The love essence is the healing Balm of Gilead. It is there to heal you my friend. Are you envious, bitter, disappointed, disillusioned or perhaps forsaken and disliked? Perhaps you are so low that you seem unable to lift yourself anymore.

[Jeremiah 8:22] Is there no balm in Gilead? Is there no physician there? Why then has not the health of the daughter of my people been restored?

The physician is writing for you right now and he presents you with the healing essence of God's love.

Please try to understand the following sentences.

Sentence one:

Jesus said, [John 16:27] **The Father Himself loves you, because you have loved Me** and have believed that I came forth from the Father.

The 'because' is very important for it implies reason as to explain why the Father loves you. Jesus said that 'He loves you because you love Me and have believed that I came from the Father.' If you associate yourself with the one the Father loves; He will also love you; that love is miraculous. God created the entire universe with the same power. And then He crowned His creation by making you and me. However, if one acts in selfishness, to the point of envy, no association is possible and the result can be loneliness and bitterness. The former creation with the pre-Adamic people were neither depraved nor evil, they were just the field (Matthew 13:38). But the moment the new creation's genes impacted that other genetic pool; starting with Cain in Nod (Asshur in Sumer, Numbers 24:22); evil had power. Wars were organized and Cain's descendant, Tubal-Cain—besides making farming tools—he also made weapons. Cain's intelligence (who was God's son just as Adam was, Luke 3:38) spawned many other things, like giving people the value of gold. With Cain came weapons, wars, the love of gold, territoriality and the general technological development.

The clash between Kenites (Genesis 15:19 & Numbers 24:20-21) and Sumerians produced giants. As a result there were evil (violent), but also gentle giants. The second kind came through the connection of Seth with women of the old creation. As these genes clashed giants were born and later, due to inbreeding they disappeared. However, their genes also run in our DNA. We have genes impacted by evil as well by God's love. In this maze of genes we have plenty to choose from. God left all up to us. So choose life. Choose wellbeing. Choose Him.

The Bible does not trace Cain's hereditary line, but only the good one through Seth. Hence, since Seth's son Enoch, people started to call on the name of the LORD (Gen. 4:26).

NOTE: Is it accidental that verse 26 coincides with the numerical value twenty-six, which is God's name YHVH? Later we will shortly go into the Bible codes.

So when Jesus told those with whom He conversed; that they are not from Abraham (genealogical line traced from Adam and Seth), but from the devil; He spoke of birth and ancestry. That devil was Cain who was the first murderer as far as we know from the Bible, as well as the first liar. (Read John 8:44 and 1John 3: 6-8 combining it with verse 12).

Conclusively and logically we see that we can only recognize Cain and Kenites—those who walk in his shoes—by their fruits (Matthew 7:16-23). The passed down to us—through Cain and his descendants' power of evil—is thus traced. Why power? Just as I have mentioned earlier, Cain gave his divine genes to Sumerians. As the first impact upon these people empires like Egypt, Assyria, Babylon and Persia also arose; followed by Greece and Rome.

How much of the Kenite you have in your genome depends on the priorities in your life as well as your choices. Remember, that unless you become like a child you cannot see and much less enter the Kingdom of God.

That is the reason why Jesus was not born a king in a most magnificent palace, but in a crib, among animals. God's kingdom comes to us in form of a tiny seed, even the mustard seed.

Although we know very little about Kenites (the word Kenite is mentioned ten times in the Bible); we recognize their fruits in others as well as in ourselves.

Many people walk about bitter being disappointed... wanting to be loved, but that love seems to be far away. In such cases the love essence, like perfumed oil seems to touch 'someone else' instead of 'me'...

Self cannot be blessed for too long. Love must be shared; it must flow for if it does not flow; then it must die or it moves elsewhere. Self actually kills or pushes love away. No liquid ever climbs, but always seeks lower places to flow into.

To some it is given to believe, while to others this very gift remains a mystery. Since the Father has chosen you and you have responded by permitting yourself to indeed be chosen, with that choice you have taken the responsibility to follow through.

Not all respond to divine election, many refuse and fight it. Many walk through this life miserable, maintaining the self-reliant and self-important stance. Such never realize, nor do they care to even think clearly that they did not come to be by their own choice, and that the 'own' plays no role whatsoever.

Many, upon seeing wonders God performs through me, 'accused' me of being anointed saying, "Oh it's just an anointing." They do not know of what spirit they are, as if anointing can easily be duplicated, manufactured and bought with money. Poor souls.

This happened after a girl came to me, straight from the street, and told me that her father was profusely bleeding suffering from cancer of the intestines. I told her to bring me his favored garment. She quickly ran home and brought her father's shirt. Again she ran to the front.

I interrupted my speech and laid hands on the garment. I sent her home telling her to give it to her father. That very moment the man's bleeding stopped. As soon as he gathered extra strength he went for medical examination. No trace of cancer was found.

This happened in San Antonio Texas, but that's just one example out of hundreds. I do not operate in faith, but in God's love. Since I please Him, I know, He tells me what and when to act. The conduit between Him and me is love, which His firstborn Son came to establish.

[John 14:12] Truly, truly, I say to you, he who believes in Me, the works that I do, he will do also; and greater works than these he will do; because I go to the Father.

None chose to be born, and none have the right to remove themselves from this life, no matter how miserable one may feel; yet that misery can be changed. So, give yourself the permission to be elected and loved.

Sentence two:

[John 6:44] No one can come to Me unless the Father who sent Me draws him...

One must be His seed and not a superficially converted-into-a-sheep wolf. One must not be just a hireling or slave, but His son or daughter and in heaven there are no earthly gender types.

The seed, tares and field speak of: His Seed (the plus) the Tares—followers and imitators of Cain's ways (the minus) and the Field—the masses (neutral).

As already said, to some it is given from above to experience God's love, while to others it seems to be denied. We find no fairness in it but discrimination.

Things are as they are and we must concur with this fact through better understanding. Love is never fair, it chooses and it is chosen; it clings to some while it avoids others. God is not fair, but righteous. You may not like it, but again, things are as they are. You are not God and you did not create the world; He did. Think about it...

[Exodus 33:19] I will be gracious to whom I will be gracious, and will show compassion on whom I will show compassion.

In other words He said; 'I will love whomever I will love.' It is My business.' We must learn the reasons behind these statements. Draw near to Me. Study Me. Find out why.

[James 4:8] As you draw near to Me I will draw near to you.

There is something for me to do, all on my own, from my will, from the already installed in me ability to choose.
This choosing act is the acceptable sacrifice, which results in Him drawing closer to me. He is God, not I. He made me, I did not make Him; if I did, I would have made a pagan idol just the way I'd like it.
Yes, we do still worship idols today almost every Sunday. That idol is called theology, for when higher knowledge comes, and greater revelation of Him we quickly choose our own idol. We love our theology more than Him.
We settled already who God is. Like a motionless picture we framed and hung Him on the wall. Quite gratified we point people to Him. We can shoot chapters, verses and sound very smart... We nailed Him down. Too often we point people not to God, but to the picture frame itself, which is supposed to hold Him, religion. But God is living, therefore moving, just as we live, move and exist, but in Him (Acts 17:28).

We tend to only portray that particular idol of the agreed upon and the well-organized belief or a dogma.

People yearn for the living and the ever-enfolding magnitude of God's love. Someone must experience it and then feed it to His children, in total liberty, in which love thrives.

Today, those same people who saw the works of power God performed through me in their midst; disagree with my theology, which according to them I have developed. No, I have developed no theology. I have not studied just God's Word, but above all, God Himself. I did not develop anything, no thesis and no theory, which then I would have to back up.

Fear rules, yet they claim to have faith. They talk about God's love yet they fear. What do they fear? There is no good sermon without the mentioning of Satan, the devil or the enemy. That is the source of fear. The Halloween type of superstition rules; mixture rules for they know not the essence of God's love. I am unleashing this flow right now.

Read sentence three:

[John 10:17-18] For this reason the Father loves Me, because I lay down My life so that I may take it again. No one has taken it away from Me, but I lay it down on My own initiative. I have authority to lay it down, and I have authority to take it up again. This commandment I received from My Father.

In God's universe everything has a reason, just as in the Holy Land every city, town and village bears a meaningful name; like Capernaum (Kfar Nahum) or Gethsemane (Gath Shmani).

One means the Village of Nahum and the other Garden of the oil press. Solomon (Shlomo), his name actually means peace and as his name was so was he. Samuel (Shmuel) means, let us hear God.

Jerusalem (Yerushalaim or Ir Shalom) means, the city of peace, etc. Therefore, in the above sentence we see that there was a reason why the Father loves His Son. The reason was that Ben Adam (Son of Man or human being) was going to do something completely on His own. "Because I lay down My life... but I lay it down on My own initiative." The Ben Elohim, the Son of God was completely subordinated to the Father and could not do anything of Himself, or on His own initiative (John 5:19; 30). Jesus did not anything on His own when it comes to power, words and miracles. But when it came to loving you and me the Ben Adam subdued his pride. Already then crucified His ego for you and me and then of His own volition laid down His life.

Jesus received a commandment, which He chose to obey, all on His own, without compulsion. God hates even your tithe or an offering when these are given under pressure or religious obligatory pressure.

Moses was commanded to take up an offering for the Lord to build the tabernacle, but He was specific about it. Moses was told to raise it but only from those whose hearts moved to give, willingly and joyfully. In the same way Apostle Paul said that giving under compulsion (2Corinthians 9:7)—like after a long fund-raising pitch—is not pleasing to the Lord. What's missing? The residential in our hearts love. Love is the motive behind any good deed for the Lord and His kingdom. Therefore, God looks for that residential in our hearts love, which is always mixed with faith.

In the last days, love will grow cold; Scripture declares (Matthew 24:12). And in Luke 18:8 Jesus said, when the Son of Man comes, will He find faith on the earth? Love will grow cold and faith will be hard to find, for faith abides together with love.

Today it is evident that any love for God is but chilly. People are ashamed to mention God in public. Yet, it was once fashionable to mention God in public during the US founding fathers era.

Sentence four:

[Matthew 5:44-46] But I say to you, love your enemies and pray for those who persecute you, so that you may be sons of your Father who is in heaven; for He causes His sun to rise on the evil and the good, and sends rain on the righteous and the unrighteous. For if you love those who love you, what reward do you have? Do not even the tax collectors do the same?

The world is already loved. The sun shines and rain falls on all, but only some are called to an exclusive walk with God. Even to love their enemies. And as the standard of God's love, one carries the healing essence of love. Whoever encounters such a carrier one begins to bathe in that healing essence of love and gradually such is being restored. The "enemy" thinking then ceases to be an enemy. The residing in you love-essence; like the Healing Balm of Gilead heals the enmity illness.

Most people draw satisfaction from the fact that whatever they do is for their children. The future of their own flesh and blood; but don't all animals do the same, from fish, birds and mammals? What's so great about doing something that nature instinctively dictates to us? If you leave your fortune to your posterity then what's so special about it? Who dares to be different? The one to whom God entrusted priceless pearls struggles. Time is ticking taking strength away, while another bathes in something moths eat and thieves can steal. Only those teachable ones and those who want to rise higher and become indeed His glorious overcomers will choose something that does not necessarily come to them naturally. In order to acquire nature divine, one must study it and concur with its higher laws. What follows is the first fruit of the Holy Spirit, (it is written as the 9th) which is self-discipline.

***

Chapter 5

THE NINE FRUITS

The nine fruits of the Holy Spirit (Galatians 5:22-23) are the nine planks on Jacob's ladder; the lowest is self-control or self-discipline. The root is self-discipline, which will eventually lead to the crowning experience. We are climbing the ladder from the earthly; the lowest and up to the top, and all the way up to the first, love. After self-control comes gentleness, for one must control oneself in order to extract gentleness. Everyone is already gentle with him or herself; the next exercise is to be gentle with everyone. The next fruit is faithfulness. As before the root fruit of self-control must be used again in order to maintain faithfulness.

In the name of something greater than the self it takes an effort to climb higher.

The next fruit is goodness. As above, to be good the act of goodness must be demonstrated, therefore chosen. To be bad is easy, for one does not need to climb the ladder, but slide down on it. One does not pay an electric bill for the usage of darkness, which is no energy at all. We pay for energy and light, which can be quite costly. Just as we discipline ourselves to work and provide, the same is with the seeking of God's kingdom.

The next fruit is kindness or compassion. It is also an act, which God uses to heal. The gift of healing manifests itself in compassion. *Jesus felt compassion for the people and He healed their sick* (Matthew 14:14).

The next fruit is patience. Again it takes self-discipline to be patient, especially with those slower ones. Temperament is a good thing, but it must be harnessed and curbed when it comes to dealings with people.

We study human IQ and each time we study it we discover new things. Things are not settled or defined yet; actually they never will be.

The next fruit is peace, which all the previous fruits have helped to create. Peace is also bestowed.

[John 14:27] Peace I leave with you; My peace I give to you; not as the world gives do I give to you. Do not let your heart be troubled, nor let it be fearful.

The world offers no security. Actually the more insecure we feel the better we can fool our opponents with the same. However, when we gain the true security, of which Jesus spoke, we then possess the true reality and then we will never trust the earthly illusions of security.

No gift or fruit works independently from our will. It is indeed a cooperation of the most exquisite kind. This cooperation leads to an absolute happiness.

The next fruit is joy, and joy is of the happy kind. By then one has outgrown self-discipline for one has established a pattern of thought, emotion and behavior, which became the outward fruit. Now, one begins to enjoy the joy of which Jesus spoke.

[John 15:11] These things I have spoken to you so that My joy may be in you, and that your joy may be made full.

Joy made full means fullness of life, happiness and contentment. Completeness. It is the perfect joy, which comes to you from heaven. It is so complete and perfect that nothing can no longer contest it nor take away.

The final fruit is the crowning experience of being loved, bathing in love and giving love. God is Love, even the Perfect Love, which extrudes from its presence doubt, timidity, uncertainty and any ulterior or dishonest motives.

In this volume I gather these particles, which point back to the Creator, and concentrate them here into one unit. By now you see that cooperation is necessary in order to become holy, which means to be set apart, dedicated to one thing only, even exclusive.

Is God a respecter of a person? As earlier said, the answer is clearly YES. God is a respecter of a person in the sense that we, as His sons in heaven, were with Him while He created the Universe. When we, His children, (the good seed in reference to Matthew 13:38) arrive on this planet—born in different lands, cultures and to different races—we find ourselves as if on a discovery tour. We study this world looking at it like through a window. If you have that kind of a feeling you must be His seed and you never felt entirely at home on this planet.

* * *

Chapter 6

HOLY, SET APART, EXCLUSIVE

We preach the Good News to all creation for the witness, for we know not who is who. We simply obey the great commission. We are here on this planet to overcome and triumph thus Give the Creator glory. That is the true purpose of this earth's sojourning.

Rain falls on the righteous and the unrighteous. Sun shines on all, but then comes the season of sprouting, growth, fruitfulness and harvest. By then we know who is who.

The discovery, as to who we are, comes in a package containing different sets of desires, longings and priorities in life, but above all the greatest and inner longing is always for love.

The search for happiness and real love, in many forms, stems from that great root of love—the Creator Himself. We see His love even in the threshing tectonic plates.

We see that our lives are fragile, indeed like grass, which lives today and is burned up the next day. We are sojourners on this planet for a reason and this reason I explain in all of my books.

[Job 38:19-21] Where is the way to the dwelling of light? And darkness, where is its place, that you may take it to its territory and that you may discern the paths to its home? You know, for you were born then, and the number of your days is great!

[Job 38:7] When the morning stars sang together and all the sons of God shouted for joy?

Yes, we were there with Him, bundled in His love, spiritually of course. We witnessed the creation as He channeled His creativity through the Firstborn Son Jesus, Yeshua. But we as those born after Yeshua, His siblings had only watched. We were only souls then. Today we have bodies.

Sentence five:

[John 17:24] Father, I desire that they also, whom You have given Me, be with Me where I am, so that they may see My glory which You have given Me, for You loved Me before the foundation of the world.

The love between the Father and His firstborn Son is most special. Those in heaven: angels, His overcomers and His sons do not share in that special kind of love. The most special love is between God-the-Spirit and those in earthly bodies today. What we learn here we cannot learn in heaven. It is this choice I am ponding upon, which God is after and it pleases Him greatly when we choose Him above all else. This repeated choice leads to a total surrender at which point God takes us just as He did take Enoch.

The loving sacrifice of Jesus, of His own self-identity and His own human will, created something new. The Father and His firstborn Son shared this love before the world came to be; and that sharing is the very essence of love. Without sharing, love is nonexistent.

If Islam maintains that God is no Father for He has no Son then the people of Allah share no love and perhaps there is the problem that can still be corrected. God loves you my dear Muslim brother and sister, and I love you, because His great love resides in me, not for me alone, but also for you.

I find it most incredible, and my spirit immensely rejoices in this statement. Jesus did not only ask the Father to reveal His and His Son's glory, but also to share the same love they have always shared.

In John 17:26 He speaks about the same love essence, which resides in the Father and the Son and circulates between them. He asks the Father that now this love would also flow out into His disciples and then through them on to us.

We are about to take hold of this love and then share it so that it can circulate between the writer and the reader.

Sentence six:

[John 3:16] For God so loved the world that He gave His only begotten Son, that whoever believes in Him shall not perish, but have eternal life.

God loves the world, the Field, for in it He hid His special treasure. He buys the world (the field) just to gain the 'mineral rights' and then dig out the temporarily hidden (or lost) treasure. As His children, we were with Him before the foundation of the Universe, but we lost that original heavenly identity, for we have allowed the affairs of this physical world to steal it from us. As a result we were lost—only to be found; we were blind—only to receive sight later on.

Through these losses comes the gracious receipt of knowledge as to who we have been all along; and only now we embrace this knowledge and bathe in our Father's love.

Enoch, before God took him alive, had the inner witness that he was pleasing to God (Hebrews 11:5). God's pleasure was in Enoch. The essence of love flowed between God and Enoch. That love had become more intense until the two blended and became one.

[John 14:23] Jesus answered and said to him, "If anyone loves Me, he will keep My word; and My Father will love him, and We will come to him and make Our abode with him.

The "We" expression speaks volumes. Before any father can have more children He enjoys the firstborn above all lavishing most affection on His Son.

From Egypt's firstborns to Moses and the entire Law, God 'pounds' on us so that we would get it. Cain did not even try to repent but willingly left Eden where God's presence was by turning his back to God.

From Your face I will be hidden (Genesis 4:14). In the old Hebrew God's face speaks of His presence. When we read the Aaronic Benediction (Numbers 6:22-26) the lifting of His face means to elevate us into His presence, to His realm, and to be close. God wants to walk among us. And when He comes closer the supernatural takes place (Leviticus 26:11-12).

So the Father's longing for all firstborn sons became all the more intense after Adam's firstborn turned his back to God.

[Genesis 4:16] Then Cain went out from the presence of the LORD, and settled in the land of Nod, east of Eden.

Not only Moses was exposed to it, but also Jesus who gave us one of His greatest parables—about the prodigal son.

Sentence seven:

[Ephesians 1-3-5] Blessed be the God and Father of our Lord Jesus Christ, who has blessed us with every spiritual blessing in the heavenly places in Christ, just as He chose us in Him before the foundation of the world, that we would be holy and blameless before Him. **In love** He predestined us to adoption, as sons through Jesus Christ to Himself, according to the kind intention of His will.

This adoption has something to do with redemption, which speaks of payment and possession. Since Jesus already paid for us, He comes back to possess that which He already paid for. This is the knowledge of our adoption as sons (genderless). As we dig deeper we realize that, as His eternal seed, we are here to discover God's love and draw it again just as Enoch did.

* * *

Chapter 7

DRAWING THE LOVE ESSENCE

One can quite easily draw the essence of His love by doing something that relates to the residence of that essence. How can we draw that love to ourselves?

At this point it becomes quite intimate, and I for one, do not want to set myself as any standard as to how one should experience it, because there are no wrongs in that experience. And for two, no one can tell you what is the correct experience because that would be dictatorship, which leads to the elimination of freedom.

Everyone will experience God's love differently and in different dimensions. Yes, there are dimensions and measures of His love. All I do is open the possibilities.

[John 17:26] (...) The love with which You loved Me may be in them, and I in them.

"The love with which You loved me" means not the love everyone already experiences, it is indeed that love you hope for and perhaps even dream about. In the heart of hearts it is indeed this love and not just sex, which climaxes and then it's over. God's love keeps spiritual climax alive.

The body is satisfied... or perhaps not yet completely, (it depends on the lovers' compatibility) and keeps on longing for more of that same pleasure. No, my friend, this is not what you really long for. You only enjoy its offshoots.

Any fleshly, soulish and sensual pleasures must be repeated like eating and drinking because they are temporary. God's love grows and increases each day.

[Psalms 16:11] You will make known to me the path of life; in Your presence is fullness of joy; in Your right hand there are pleasures forever.

There is no match for the eternal or endless pleasures He wants you to experience. He is there when you love your wife or your husband. He is at your breakfast table and at sundown.

God introduces Himself not as a wrathful God, but as a God of relationship. He is abounding in loving-kindness, which speaks of an overflow. He may put on a garment of wrath, but then He takes it off and hangs it on a hook, but the essence of His being, His love remains.

Atheists want you to accept their belief in nothing, (atheism is not necessarily any absence of faith, but rather a faith placed in something else); saying that this God of anger who condones the murder of women and children; and who permits wars and atrocities is nonexistent. Yet facts remain. We choose and do what we want on this planet, we are gods. Cain was a god because according to the definition he heard God.

[John 10:34-36] Jesus answered them, "Has it not been written in your Law, 'I SAID, YOU ARE GODS'? [35] If he (Moses) called them gods, to whom the word of God came (and the Scripture cannot be broken) [36] do you say of Him, whom the Father sanctified and sent into the world, 'You are blaspheming,' because I said, 'I am the Son of God'?"

Cain received the word (Gen. 4:7) he even conversed with God person to person, and yet he disobeyed and learned nothing. Then this divinity went on to the people who were only a field. All of a sudden many of them became the Tares.

The misuse of the precious gift of God draws severe consequences. Many today are under God's wrath and that is the reason why they became atheists.

[Exodus 20:5-6] (...) I am a jealous God, visiting the iniquity of the fathers on the children, on the third and the fourth generations of those who hate Me, [6] but showing lovingkindness to thousands, to those who love Me and keep My commandments.

[Exodus 34:6-7] Then the LORD passed by in front of him and proclaimed, "The LORD, the LORD God, compassionate and gracious, slow to anger, and abounding in lovingkindness and truth; [7] who keeps lovingkindness for thousands, who forgives iniquity, transgression and sin; yet He will by no means leave the guilty unpunished, visiting the iniquity of fathers on the children and on the grandchildren to the third and fourth generations."

We have been taught that God loves all people; He loves the entire world. That is true. He loves the world for the sake of the treasure He found in the field (the world the masses).

At the end of time there will be the selection of the good fish and the bad ones (parables), the sheep and the goats, the chaff and the wheat, etc. Why? He is only after some. He loves whom He loves, He chooses whom He chooses and you cannot change it. You can wander in circles defining yourself, but God is God. He is not a human being, no matter how much you would like Him to be one. Period.

[Exodus 34:6] The LORD, the LORD God, compassionate and gracious, slow to anger, and abounding in lovingkindness and truth.

Atheists feel very righteous in what they say; concluding that they do not want to believe in such a God. They avoid other passages of scripture that state that we have the power and the responsibility to rule the earth righteously.

We are the rulers over this planet having the choice to make war or promote peace.

The entire Bible teaches us what being righteous means. What is a righteous rule and what is unrighteous, what moral is and what is immoral. Yet, hardly any of these questions are being considered. Blame is easy and usually originates in self-righteousness, which God does not have, for He looks after our needs, both physical as well as spiritual. He watches us. He sends us teaching, but in order to receive teaching one must be willing to learn.

Look how easy it is to kill another human being. One perhaps wishes that this ability should not be given to us. Or if God exists He would have prevented all killing. Then that would mean we are not human beings but robots.

Yet, He says, that after this period of tests on this planet the former things will be erased as if they have never existed. Therefore the three types of people on earth serve as furnishings for the good seed. Like a rocket boosters they are ejected, burn up in the atmosphere and are no more; no hell, no torment, no eternal sufferings...

After the field and tares have finished their mission on earth they will be erased from existence. Our view of righteousness and fairness has nothing to do with God's righteousness. When those we knew, even liked; will not show up in heaven we will know that they have been erased. They won't have the time to open their mouths and say ah. Actually you and I will not even know them at all for those memories will also be erased. The forward-moving time will be rolled into eternity back into no time; and with it all former memories will be gone. Just as our sins, when confessed in repentance, are completely erased, as if they have never been committed, so it will be with the Tares and the Field. Every tear, every ache and hurt will be remembered no more for the former things, of the present dispensation of time, will come to an end. However, what will remain is the overcomer.

The victors took this dispensation of time to become much more than what nature tells them to do. They have even loved their enemies, even the murderers and rapists and all abominable people, shining light divine also into their lives. But looking from God's viewpoint it is hard to separate the sinner from his sin. In the flood both the sinner and his sin had perished. So the only way we can love our enemy is to heal them of the enmity malady. But to love a murderer, child molester or a rapist, and at the same time hate his sin; from God's viewpoint is not possible. So why should I try to be better than God? Unless God reveals to me otherwise I leave such cases in God's hands. I do not know. I remain neutral but I am still God's light; God standard of love; whoever comes to me can be healed.

In mid 80's somewhere in the Midwest (I think that this prison was called Pacifica in either Missouri or Illinois) I was once invited to a state prison. At first, when I passed through that prison's gates I felt a bit intimidated. I was never before inside a prison.

There were about 50 prisoners hearing me preach. I made an invitation to come to Jesus. No one budged. But after a while a very thin man on the top bench raised his hand. Very slowly he was helped down to where I was. In those days AIDS was not yet known. The man was just skin and bones and he could hardly stand. He gave his life to God through the Lord Jesus. I prayed for healing of his emaciated body. He responded and was instantly energized. With that new strength he went up back to his seat. I sang and played guitar and many joined me in the chorus.

On the next day, the leader of the group who brought me to that place told me that the man was completely healed. He worked up a great appetite and started to gain weight. A couple of weeks later I was told that the man started a Bible group. Eventually all those who heard me preach joined the group and one by one all of them gave their lives to God. They saw this incredible miraculous transformation in that dying man and they could not help but to acknowledge, not only the existence of God, but also His presently working power.

So I do not know as to who is who. The rain falls on all, which is the Gospel of Truth. Then I recognize the hidden, even the lost seed coming to me. The Seed is gathered together and stored in God's barn, but although the Tares will be also bundled together they will be burned up.

God picked up just one and through this dying man He changed many.

Had I remained intimidated I could not think about those criminals, but only about my own feelings. But I laid my life down. God's love asks for it.

On my way out, to my surprise, many showed me that love and gratitude. With happy smiles they sent me off waving.

* * *

THE GOD ESSENCE

Ever since that day my opinion about criminals has changed. Seeing them as blind, lame and lost can only be accomplished through God's love.

Love is never selfish. Love is of the selfless essence. But why do we see so little of it? It's because of greed and the unleashed desire to profit from any given opportunity. None want to open up the inner storehouse of love, lest one be taken for a ride, used or abused and then dumped.

The essence of love exists, but it is neatly packaged and marketed. Novels and movies keep the hunger alive, but none satisfy it for if they did the cash flow would then cease.

You do not want the worldly peace; you want the real one. You do not want the worldly joy but again, the real one. In the same way, you do not want to eat something packaged and conserved having years of shelf life, but the ever fresh, living and eternal love of God.

God introduces Himself to Moses on Mt Sinai as: compassionate and gracious, slow to anger, abounding in lovingkindness and truth; who keeps lovingkindness for thousands, who forgives iniquity, transgression and sin.

After Moses was thus introduced, God wanted His servant to pass it on to His people. Moses, indeed had a hard job, for how can you teach the ex-slaves that God is love? "What were we doing in Egypt for 430 years serving the Egyptians? Oh God, where were You all this time?"

To agree the flesh with spiritual things is impossible. The pride of the physical life is indeed powerful, yet very necessary. This pride works with self-identity, which again, can only be fleshly and never spiritual. Spiritual beings have no self-identity but the Creator's. God will change anyone who submits his or her earthly identity to Him.

Do I see any profit in surrendering my will to God the Father? Tremendous. The self-identity and pride must be first broken before one could extract God's love and have an experience with it; and in order to do that there must be a mechanism that does it. That mechanism, which God used, was actually the Egyptian slavery. After humbling the Hebrew pride, God had better chances in showing His love; and so the Israelites had better chances in experiencing it. The humbling is nothing else than making a hollow vessel out of a lump of clay. A lump of clay is no vessel at all; so, it must be formed to the point of becoming hollow then it can hold the essence of God's love.

The purpose of this writing is to bring you to the point of understanding. Once you make the decision to humble this crazy pride of life before Him by seeking Him, then His love will show up.

Some are moved by the fear of God or the fear of punishment. Others are moved by God's compassion and love. By knowing this well, God incorporated these three types of people into one. The Field, which was the bulk of the people; the Tares, which were the lovers of gold, self and power, great warriors—these were working the hardest to be someone on earth. In this process the Tares equipped God's Seed.

Today publically traded companies seek nothing else but only profits. They are under pressure. They must perform for winning has become the corporate god.

Quite naturally the sons respond to the Father's love without much teaching or splitting of hairs, while others had to be organized, and as it were, locked into some ritual religious gridlock and threatened with eternal fires of hell. However, God's sons hear their Father's voice and obey it without any duress. They hear His voice only when He speaks, they don't imagine Him speak, but hear Him in truth. God does not speak every single day nor is He obligated to. His prophets did not hear Him for years until He spoke. They even specified the period in which God spoke.

In His kingdom pretense does not exist because His kingdom is completely governed by His truth.

The Spirit searches all things even the deepest depths and the highest heights. Nothing's hidden in His realm, for only in darkness something can hide. God's realm is filled to the brim with the brightest of all lights. No time either, everything's instant and present.

His sons, who come from this most glorious realm, operate according to the laws of that realm, although only to a certain extent because they are also in the physical realm of time. Having bodies—subject to gravity, hunger and thirst, aches and pains, which can only be found in physical bodies—can be burdensome for indeed God speaks in a relaxed state and in peace.

* * *

Chapter 9

GOD'S TENDER MERCIES

The peace Jesus gave us, unlike the peace of this world, is the essence of the heavenly realm in which communication is never interrupted or unhindered in any way.

Here is the explanation why we are called overcomers, conquerors, those that prevail.

Either we belong to this earth and turn into dust, or we identify with the realm of the perpetual life and eventually get translated into it—glorified.

Whatever one digests, interprets and handles; one becomes. Therefore be busy with God's love only. Draw it to yourself in order to release it unto others.

No matter how wicked you might have been, as long as you can read what is being written here, you are still under God's grace.

Those who walk around with the fear of having sinned against the Holy Spirit can be assured that they have not sinned against Him because they are still live.

Ananias and Sapphira (Acts 5) did not have that chance. The moment they lied to the Holy Spirit they dropped dead, without the grace to repent, which time really is. You might have grieved the Holy Spirit, but then again, I doubt it, because in the organized religion, pious intimidation often rules as if to keep the faithful in check; even whip them into obedience. All sorts of things get told, but hardly ever out of God's love or His abundant grace, but often out of sheer frustration. I've been there myself. I can't remember how many warnings I have given. Oh yes, I had a big chip on my shoulder too; and to take it off took me a while. That chip was like a heavy beam, which I could not carry anymore.

Since I have licked a little more of truth, broke my pride and tasted God's love; I stopped that former religious nonsense. I leave all judgments to the Great Judge.

I do what He commands and my only motivation is pure love for Him. I do not hoard people into heaven because I told them about hell. If they are not His sheep, and it's not been granted them from above then they can only be labeled as sheep, but never really be one? By their fruits you will know them (Matthew 7:16-20).

[2Kings 22:19] ...because your heart was tender and you humbled yourself before the LORD.

If you are loved you will love in return, but what if you do not know yet that you are indeed loved. No one told you that you are loved; and how this love essence really works. Well, I tell you that you are loved beyond your wildest dreams. God's love is endless. The better explanation of that love is found in the next quote.

[Psalms 136] His lovingkindness is everlasting.

The entire Psalm consists of 26 verses and each verse ends with the above words. The Psalmist extols God's mercy, as it is being translated in the King James Bible, but mercy can also be understood as pity. It's much more than mercy or pity, it is loving-kindness (N. A. S. B.), which has no beginning and no end; it is endless.

The Hebrew word used for loving-kindness is CHESED. This speaks of brotherly love, protective love, even to the point of slaying the attacker in the act of defending the one He or she loves. In the Modern Hebrew CHESED is often being used for grace, which comes from another word HANNAN. To be gracious is to be HANNOON. These few modern changes help us to grasp why the psalmist used that word in Psalms 136. The context shows that CHESED motivates all of God's actions. Perhaps you have not seen God in action as I have. Even the fact that I write about it now is His and not my action.

Note verse 18, He slew mighty kings, for His lovingkindness is everlasting. The slaying does not sound like mercy or love, but in this case it is CHESED. In defense of His beloved He slays His beloved's enemy. That's my God. Would you like to know Him? For this reason we are admonished to leave all avenging to God.

[Romans 12:19] Never take your own revenge, **beloved**, but leave room for the wrath of God, for it is written, "VENGEANCE IS MINE, I WILL REPAY," says the Lord.

Note the word Paul uses, BELOVED. Make sure that you are God's beloved first. Once you know this; the rest is easy for you have become His peacemaker.

Again, the atheists have perhaps never been exposed to this sort of knowledge, for perhaps they have chosen to be rather lost in their "own" vain imaginations.

The laws set into motion by the Creator are not plainly presented, but are rather obscured on purpose for some kind of a test. While one is offended and finds basis for voiding all faith in God, another finds amazing intelligence and logic.

Let's take the Bible codes, which recently gained quite a significant attention, which also is being heavily criticized as a bunch of hogwash, but why? Some have a deep aversion to these things and combat it; as if they whispered into their mother's ear to conceive them and bring them forth; and if they have the power to take their "own" lives into their hands and do with them whatever they wish.

God is omniscient and ALL knowing, past, present and future is known to Him in minute detail. Sorry is their state, for they know nothing of living and traversing this realm purely by grace. Pride of this life indeed whips them into subordination; they are imprisoned, and actually try to snap out of this bondage, but the sacrifice seems too steep. They ejected the Creator out of His seat and seated themselves in His stead. They study but only material things, which prop up their lofty positions. That pride breeds nothing else but foolishness.

[Isaiah 43:4] Since you are precious in My sight, since you are honored and I love you, I will give other men in your place and other peoples in exchange for your life.

In September 1939 in today's Belarus my father was drafted into the Polish army. He prayed that he might not even touch a weapon let alone be trained to kill. What a poor soldier he would have made, but God answered his prayer.

My father was not too tall, so he was placed at the end of the line. When the weapons were being distributed and the sergeant finally reached the 'shorty' he embarrassingly said, "It's funny, but we seem to have run out of rifles." Later, they gave him a bayonet and that was the best they could do. That was strange. What would 'shorty' do with a long knife; pierce tanks?

My father was then sent to the frontlines and that's when he threw the bayonet away. Those who saw him wondered why no bullet or shrapnel had ever touched him. They thought that perhaps the man is some kind of an angel.

Many joined up with my father for he seemed extremely lucky. And just as it is at a casino's roulette table where people bet on the winner so they tried the same with my father.

Together they ran to safety under heavy shelling. I vividly remember how he described the machine gun shooting; the whistling bullets and scattered shrapnel. He fell and ran, fell and ran until he realized that no one else ran with him anymore. None ever made it... except the one, my father. Again, he was left alone without a scratch. God kept him alive, so that I might be born and tell you about God's love and its awesome power.

This booklet is only an appetizer; for what I have in store for you, is mindboggling. Do I want you to get it all? - Of course.

Do I want to sell? No! I'd prefer to be wealthy and give it all for free, but I am not. There is marketing involved and if I give it all for free only a few would receive it; and what about others? In order to spread anything around, others must be rewarded for their time and efforts; so naturally, people's jobs depend on it. What about months and years spent writing? I must pay bills, eat and rest in a comfortable bed. Most of my life I ate strange foods and slept in strange beds. What about millions out there? Don't you want to open the gates of God's love also for them?

Unlike the reality on earth, where love seems to evaporate over time the essence divine gets better with time; more intense. For a very long time Enoch walked with God. God was pleased and Enoch felt it. Of course, this union of joy and delight is not natural. Yes, it is supernatural and I already enjoy it. I lead you to it with many words addressing the love essence from many angles. Our vocabulary is too poor.

What's great on the earth is as nothing in heaven. Whatsoever becomes proud on this planet—often made so through the accumulation of wealth, high position or some prestigious social standing—in God's eternal kingdom means absolutely nothing.

***

Chapter 9

THE LAST IS FIRST AND THE FIRST IS LAST

The laws of physics are for this earth and they cannot ever be mixed up with the gravitation-less, instantaneous and timeless sphere of the spiritual realm. What belongs to earth is only material and what belongs to heaven is spiritual.

The Tares have life and the Good Seed; but the earth's dust, the Field (people), is purely material. Although life elements impregnated the earth and all plants, yet if you take life out of these you have only a dead and lifeless matter. Symbolically, these are compared to people inhabiting this planet. However, the life God speaks of is not the life that makes birds fly, fish swim or lions hunt.

Life is most precious for it is laden with God's essence of love. We enjoy nature because we enjoy love. Lions kill and tear apart an herbivore; their faces drenched in blood. We like to see a living lion, but not an eating one; we pity its prey because life has just exited it to sustain another.

[Deuteronomy 22:6-7] If you happen to come upon a bird's nest along the way, in any tree or on the ground, with young ones or eggs, and the mother sitting on the young or on the eggs, you shall not take the mother with the young; you shall certainly let the mother go, but the young you may take for yourself, in order that it may be well with you and that you may prolong your days.

The temporary and transitional life, which resides in all creatures, works on a totally different principle than the Spirit of Life. The vivifying force of life in all creatures sustains only the physical enclosures, in which divine life may reside. Divine life can only be found in humans, never in animals, plants, fish or birds. The Spirit of Life does not work on the premise of self-preservation, but the opposite—self-relinquishment.

Once we get attached to the Spirit and He impregnates our being we grasp this concept of no beginning and no end. The world calls it as something abstract, but it is not abstract, it is a between realm. If you could pin it down then you could control it. Life must be sustained at any cost. God's Spirit of Life carries His tender mercies, which are in plural because they are endless.

The following verses deal with the perpetual nature of life; propagated by love and mercy.

Obviously the reader is encouraged to understand the underlying motives. One can take the eggs, but not together with the mother bird, because the mother can lay more eggs and produce offspring. If one takes the mother, the eggs won't hatch. If one takes her young then the mother bird has still a chance to reproduce, but if one takes the mother bird then her chicks will die from starvation. In some cases another bird adopts the eggs until they hatch.

The Compassionate One shows His tenderness by teaching us how to care for life, for indeed we are stewards of this planet. Isn't that enough to see God for who He really is? Could Moses alone come up with these sayings? He was indeed with God's love, which is why he said, "Since I found favor in your eyes…"

[Exodus 33:12-13] "You have said, 'I have known you by name, and **you have also found favor in My sight.**' Now therefore, I pray You, if I have found favor in Your sight, let me know Your ways that I may know You."

Only by the sheer power of that favor could Moses write what he wrote. He also showed anger and frustration and accepted punishment and he wrote about that too. No man can write such things as if sucking it all out of his thumb, unless God overshadowed him and gave him the right sense about God's Kingdom. The invisible to the natural eyes kingdom operates on the law of love; and its breathing essence is again, love. Take a whiff of it now.

The Bible is the only book that does not glorify its writers, but rather its writers seem to be quite self-critical. Who in their right mind would write that God had exiled us for we were bad? A stranger reads Israel's History Book (the Bible) and throws it back at the Jewish descendant saying, "Aha, I read in your book that God had rejected you."

In the Bible we find war and peace, the right and wrong and not one man's blind indoctrination as is the case with other books. The Bible gives you the ammunition to hate its writers or love them. Their efforts in the preservation of the biblical texts are most remarkable. The Qumran caves and the Dead Scrolls bear witness to this fact; for the 2,000-years old Book of Isaiah, for example, is almost verbatim the same as the one we read today but transcribers and copiers died horrible deaths.

[Exodus 23:19] You are not to boil a young goat in the milk of its mother.

Have mercy, o man. Understand life and its true essence. How could anyone take a newborn kid, then milk of its mother, and then throw that kid into that milk and boil it? That milk is meant for the newborn and not to satisfy one's heartless greed. Yes, tender mercies.

Life is precious. Children feel it. Adults somehow lose that sense, but wish to be innocent again. That choice has never been taken away from you. Choose!

Only an adult can become like a child again. Children cannot become adults for their will largely belongs to their parents. God expects of us to use the power of choice and decision, which love and care represent. Once you decide to practice it, in spite of any disappointments and personal hurts, you will draw the love essence to yourself.

God wants to be sought because of the resident in Him love, which like a river must flow somewhere. Angels bathe in it all the time, but do not appreciate it because they do not experience its opposites. In the ream of contrasts appreciation is possible, but again that also must be chosen and expressed. Angels act automatically on God's love, having no will of their own; they do not have to choose it.

It was given to us to eat of the Tree of Knowledge and between the knowledge of good and evil we choose one or the other; even choose to repent and return to our Maker. This very contrast, indeed, produces choice; but instead, religion taught us to bemoan the fact that we (Adam & Eve) supposedly fell. As if an accident occurred in God's timeless kingdom. The same God who showed Daniel the successive kingdoms, could not foresee Satan's plot?

The Bible can be used for blind indoctrination, but it can also be used to test us; and the God given gift of intelligence, while some now begin to use it, others sold it to the less intelligent champions of religion.

We did not fall. We transgressed God's commandment, for the Omniscient and Omnipotent Sovereign One planned it so, knowing very well that we did not have yet the contrast by which we gain the ability to choose.

The problem is not the transgression, but rather the lack of return to Him (repentance); and the humbling of pride in order to gain His brand and quality of knowledge.

It may sound shockingly new to you and someone may imply an error or even falsehood to the above statement, yet it is not false when you believe that God is Omniscient, Omnipresent and Omnipotent.

The Sovereign One indeed knew, even planned it from the very beginning, wanting us to take the journey with Him. Learn, make mistakes, fall, get up, repent and choose, love Him of your own free will. There must be at least one spark of love for God left in us; otherwise repentance will be extremely hard coming... if not ever. Repentance has not gone away from God's original drawing map. His plans still contain this wonderful ability and power to turn back to Him with one's entire heart, mind and soul. The problem was not transgression, but rather lack of repentance.

In Hebrew 'Shoov' means to turn back direction home like the prodigal son. Once this course is taken what one meets are the laden with love open arms of the Father and no lost paradise. We are not in a fallen state, but rather in a misinformed state; therefore in an unloved and lonely state.

Man's religion robbed us of this vibrant and living relationship. "Come home My son, My daughter"—says the Lord.

* * *

Chapter 10

God's plans for you

[Jeremiah 29:11-14] For I know the plans that I have for you,' declares the LORD, 'plans for welfare and not for calamity to give you a future and a hope. 'Then you will call upon Me and come and pray to Me, and I will listen to you. 'You will seek Me and find Me when you search for Me with all your heart. 'I will be found by you,' declares the LORD...

Love motivates the seeking; lack of seeking means indifference. Perhaps you are satisfied living without the love of God in your life? I am not. I hunger and thirst after Him and want more of His love. I churn milk in order to get butter. I cooperate and I seek.

How can His plans for you ever come to pass if you wouldn't care about Him or what He says? Learning His ways and the laws of His realm draws down its substance, even the essence of His love. The more you seek it the more you will experience it; and the closer it approaches; the more enjoyable your life becomes. Even as you enjoy reading this booklet, you may sense a strange joy; cotton-balls-like feeling; that's His love enveloping you. However, if you don't feel it yet, then please release your desire and longing for it. Start churning until you yourself separate the cream from buttermilk.

Enjoy His presence for He wants you to. Enjoy His prosperity in every area of your life, but let His love flow into you first. If there's something obstructing this flow, then confess it and part with it for the test of what you love more comes first.

If you love the eternal more than the temporary thrills, with which one day you will have to part—and don't want to grieve His Spirit anymore—then you are ready. The glorious love experience, which you long for, is about to flow to the valley of your need.

* * *

Chapter 11

GOD'S LOVE EXPRESSED THROUGH A MINISTRY

A ministry is a light bearer; and God's love is like a candlestick. The light becomes more and more intense and ever brighter.

[Romans 5:5] The love of God has been poured out within our hearts through the Holy Spirit who was given to us.

We would not be doing anything significant without the fuel of the Holy Spirit poured into our hearts and His fire.

A ministry must be effective in changing lives. The power of the Holy Spirit comes only to change something old into something new, otherwise we have no need for that awesome power of God.

Obviously, the Lord does not want you to be satisfied with something you already know. He wants to give you something fresh and very new, like the oven freshly baked bread. Also, the new wine must be poured but into new wineskins. Therefore the new wineskins must be made first.

[Isaiah 48:6-7] I proclaim to you new things from this time, even hidden things, which you have not known. "They are created now and not long ago; and before today you have not heard them, so that you will not say, 'Behold, I knew them.'

Tradition and repetitiousness of anything old will never produce wisdom. Inspiration comes from the Holy Spirit, but when it comes we must part with those comfortable beaten paths in which the fleshly man feels quite secure; therefore unwilling to change.

Yes, let the flesh feel insecure and let the spirit man triumph in your life. The new is always challenging and the Lord loves to bring it to us. God's love is intense and possessive. Pagans fear our "mysterious" God, because they do not know Him as the Perfect Love that eliminates *all* fears. Our God is mighty. He is your Father. He made you for Himself. You have not made Him for yourself to suit your every whim and desire.

He is the straight line, which any zigzags of yours must finally be made straight and blend with His truth. His word is the sanctifying Truth (John 17:17).

If we won't cooperate and bring forth fruits; the works of our faith; then God will. But then our love directed toward Him was not manifested, but only His love toward us. Do you understand this mutuality?

[Deuteronomy 30:6-15] The LORD your God will circumcise your heart and the heart of your descendants, to love the LORD your God with all your heart and with all your soul, so that you may live. (...) "It is not in heaven, (...) nor is it beyond the sea, (...) the word is very near you, in your mouth and in your heart, (...) to love the LORD your God, to walk in His ways.

O my dear friend, it is so simple and yet to a fleshly person it is so hard. Why being fleshly, what does one profit from being so hard, "established" in formalities and the repetitive beaten paths? – Is eating, drinking and eliminating so important that it takes over all of our attention? Money, which is added to something much higher, often becomes the most sought after commodity and the source of most worries.

You do not know what a minister has to go through when supported by people whose whims often change. If we were depending on people's support and only look into their hands we would have quit ministering long time ago. The pressure would have been unbearable. We see how people oppress themselves with the unnecessary. Although they know well about the supernatural provisions, yet, they still worry. That worry steals the very joy and blocks the very experience with God's love. We can attain to that special resting place.

The love of God, like anything else in life is released when we speak about it. It is then that we make it present. Try it my dear friend. Find someone you can exchange words about the love of God. It is not far from you it is so near; and as you read it about it right now the exchange is already taking place. Give it further. Don't keep it all to yourself for if you do you alienate it. God's love must flow. It cannot be possessed, just as you cannot possess God, but He can possess you.

If you were able to possess God's perfect Love you would be a god and you would rule the Universe. If you were able to control God's attributes, lovingkindness, compassion and the supernatural then you would control God Himself.

Many try to do exactly that. They have already demonstrated this fact in many ways; one of them is theology. A framed picture is a controlled picture of God; therefore an idol and no longer the All Mighty.

Today, I got information from one of my blogs where a man driven by the show-off force went almost crazy. This showiness is so obvious that I wanted to write back 'thanking him for showing off.' The emotional bondages are so obvious. I think that my writings pushed his buttons and the man driven by his "I know so" ego kept on spawning fragments upon fragments of his restless thoughts. Perhaps he seeks healing? But judging from what he wrote I see that his disgusting enslaving pride would not permit him to receive healing.

Pagans fear God; His children are loved by God and love Him back by sharing His love with others. If you do not know who is God's child then ask Him and He will lead you to one. Don't waste precious time on those who harbor hate, animosities and have never tried to reconcile with anyone by holding a grudge; a sign of a sick soul. Have mercy on them and move on with God's love.

No one can possess God and no one can possess His love, or hoard it up and keep it all to oneself. That selfishness tramples down those most precious pearls. God's love must be shared, from mouth to mouth, from smile to smile, from one good word to another good word; regardless if you deserve it or not. Do it for the sheer joy of sharing and giving, then experience that heavenly thrill, which everyone seeks.

I give God's love to you, and I do love you, because I am "blessedly selfish" (positive) I am blessed each time I share God's love. After you have shared God's love you would want to repeat that thrilling experience. Yes, you want to be blessed and be loved in return. There's nothing wrong with that; Jesus said that such is the law and the prophets (Matthew 22:36-38).

God made us to be pleasure-oriented people, but He has enormous reserves of divine pleasures. Since He had made us so, He wants us to experience the same from us.

The German language has already sold that word "pleasure" to just the physical experience, and that's too bad. The language symbolizes how the German-speaking people have deprived themselves of the extra-dimensional pleasurable experience with God. God has sent His love and He always uses people. But people abuse God's love, simply because their souls are not well; and in a very peculiar way do not want to get well. It's a mystery.

[Psalms 16:11] You will make known to me the path of life; in Your presence is fullness of joy; in Your right hand there are pleasures forever.

It is not a religion or religiousness, which only belongs in a church. It belongs at your family table while breaking bread, just as you share a meal together; using love-filled words share God's love. You can eat the physical food and at the same time the spiritual. That's how God's love begins to be poured into your heart and the thrill of hearing it is much more than just the hearing itself; it is the heavenly joy, which you long for.

The Holy Spirit is often portrayed as the River of Life, the Spirit of Truth, the Seal of Truth, the Word, the Person Lord Jesus, and the light.

The seven spirits of God are: (1) Fear of God, (2) Understanding, (3) Knowledge, (4) Wisdom, (5) Strength and (6) Counsel; they always come as if surrendering the (7) Holy Spirit (Isaiah 11:2). Fear of God is the beginning of wisdom, but before you become wise you must gain understanding, which absorbs knowledge. When the absorbed knowledge is practiced the result is wisdom, which is practical and applicable. Then, and only then you become strong. Only the strong can counsel. So the sixth spirit (an angel) is strength. This is the ministry of the Holy Spirit.

Presently the Holy Spirit ministers to you His Understanding and Knowledge. The moment you begin to practice what you know the Spirit of Wisdom will assist you. If you do not practice the NEW THINGS He taught you (even through this ministry) you would never become wise.

Wisdom is a deed. Only after one practices the new knowledge one then becomes wise and therefore strong. You cannot be strong without wisdom. That's just the way it is.

Only after you have become wise you can counsel others, for God is not interested in our theories, but in a proven practice.

[James 1:22] But **prove yourselves doers of the word**, and not merely hearers who delude themselves.

When the Holy Spirit comes, the truth comes also, never illusion, which is something that appears to be true, but then disappears. Illusion is a camouflaged lie.

[Isaiah 30:10] Who say to the seers, "You must not see visions"; and to the prophets, "You must not prophesy to us what is right speak to us pleasant words, prophesy illusions.

People want to please the external part of themselves and hardly ever the internal spiritual part. They only want soothing words that tell them how great they are or how great they will become. Such soothsayers prophesy illusions. This commerce nears the temple's Holy Holies. It provokes God's holy wrath, which Jesus expressed. Some churches even encourage improper behavior, but why?

[1Corinthians 13:5] Love does not act unbecomingly; it does not seek its own...

* * *

Chapter 12

CALLED OUT OF DARKNESS

A pagan acting like a pagan in a Synagogue would be most improper. A man scowling like a pig or a dog, and calling it the Holy Spirit; is most improper. Doing strange things in a meeting, like crawling on the floor or under chairs and barking like a dog; is most improper. The list is long. Bizarre behavior does not attract anyone to God's love, but does exactly the opposite, pushes God's love away.

Why people do it can be explained with one sentence: they do not know God. Yes, they are far from Him. They try to copy something spiritual and that copy is always weird and repulsive to those who do know God.

And about this Apostle Paul already spoke in the Letter to the Corinthians. The Corinthians acted out their paganism for it was very much resident within them; their 'genes' carried it. All they needed to do is to only access that department of weirdness and let themselves go. It's been in them for thousands of years, and it continues to be so to this today. All one needs is plenty of alcohol and a weird behavior is then perhaps very proper at some beer drinking party where everyone supposed to hang loose; but in God's presence it is not fitting; if indeed God's presence is there at all?

Strangely enough, the same people that have turned their backs to the truth seek to fill the void with pagan oddities and then they call it freedom in the Holy Ghost. God's love never embarrasses anyone. Love shields and protects. Holy Spirit is also the extension of God's love to us. Do you know the Holy Spirit? Do you love Him? Do you want to know Him? Do you want to love Him and be loved by Him in return?

[1Peter 4:8] Above all, keep fervent in your love for one another, because love covers a multitude of sins.

Amazing, nothing else covers sins but love. This big sin hoopla became a monster. Yet we can forgive sins and even cover them. The reason for it is that God's prophet does not need to know your secret sins because of love. His preaching and teaching should be enough. It is not allowed to publically reveal anyone's sins because of repentance, which covers, removes and drowns all sins in the depths of the sea (Micah 7:19). They are then forgotten as if they never happened.

If someone is so hardened with sin that he or she needs/wants a minister's finger directed at them telling him or her their dirty secrets, publically; and only then they would cave in; then there was never God's love in them in the first place.

I knew a lady who acted weird. A precious lady, but she could not let go of her weirdness. One day I told her, "listen, you do not need to do this in order to get attention, the word of God in your mouth gets our attention, so stop this weirdness." Her hand was shaking and she was convulsing as if the Holy Spirit is a boxer throwing punches at her stomach. This weird imagination that the Holy Spirit is something strange is pagan. The lady stopped it all at once and became quite normal. I did not take her spirituality away.

[1Peter 2:9] But you are a chosen race, a royal priesthood, a holy nation, a people for God's own possession, so that you may proclaim the Excellencies of Him who has called you out of darkness into His marvelous light (Holy Spirit).

We are royalty. We are children of the Highest. We are here to bring more glory to our Maker. We overcome and conquer because His seed abides in us. God is Spirit and He wants to indwell our huts of clay turning them into most exquisite and glorious palaces.

* * *

BORN OF LOVE

No matter how we look at our lives, one fact remains unchanged; we are born because of some form of love. How you interpret that love remains subjective.

In romance, love is being mentioned; and then a man asks a woman to marry him; and when she accepts his "invitation" they are then joined as one. Then comes the weeding, sex and pregnancy. Baby is born, a newcomer into this world—the fruit of love. Children grow up. Parents are happy in their mission of caring and providing for their offspring. They are happy serving, investing and often pouring themselves out for their children. That's how God made it all.

A similar process, and naturally so, takes place in nature. Let's look at birds. Parents provide for their chicks until the fly out of the nest.

God is compassionate, full of loving-kindness and slow to anger. He is merciful and as such He introduced Himself to Moses who had to grasp this reality and never let go. A couple thousands of years later come God's Firstborn Son and for contrast for His discourse he picks up Moses. He starts His line with, "You have heard that the ancients were told..." He speaks of the Law and then he inserts something brand new. "But I say to you..." The fifth chapter of Matthew deals with contrasts: God's love, mercy and peace.

[Matthew 5:46-48] For if you love those who love you, what reward do you have? Do not even the tax collectors do the same? If you greet only your brothers, what more are you doing than others? Do not even the Gentiles do the same? Therefore you are to be perfect, as your heavenly Father is perfect.

Doing what is acceptable in the society and doing that which nature dictates remains but earthly. In order to become sons of our Father [48] one must first study God's firstborn Son. All that Jesus said contains information about the kingdom of heaven and its everlasting properties. But what are those properties? – No time. No boundaries, and no territory, which one can possess and control. No darkness; nothing can hide therein. No double talk or ulterior motives; any hidden things are plain and known to all. No illusion, no pretense, but a completely open truth. No hate and no malice. Divine love permeates everything and every angel. Everyone in heaven reacts to the promptings of God's love.

I just mentioned few of the heavenly characteristics and can go longer yet; but I must pause, for these words serve only as inspiration and not any predigested food.

We grow older and we call it maturity, but that maturity comes to us through disappointments, hardships, hurts, injustices, and problems in school, society or in the family. We learn to shield our vulnerabilities, and coat our souls; we build the ever-thicker walls in which we seek shelter form the onslaught of troubles. But is this really maturity; can I reinterpret it for you?

[Matthew 18:3] Truly I say to you, unless you are converted and become like children, you will not enter the kingdom of heaven.

Getting reconverted into a child-like state of being takes our willingness, but that willingness for us, the "mature people", takes a business-like approach because before we "buy" it we must see some value in it. "What's in it for me?" we say.

If I'd like to sell you something here I would advertise it promising great rewards, like you becoming great, rich and very important, but that's not the advertisement God wants to give you now. We do not become like children in order to get or become someone of the earthly or the social value, but rather we become like children in order to know the Father and His ways. We become like children to taste heaven within us. If I told you that I do taste it then I would advertise and make it appetizing. I cannot sell you my anointing. I cannot give you what I have inside for if I have then the entire work of making disciples would be in vain.

[Matthew 28:10; John 15:8] Go therefore and make disciples of all the nations, (...) teaching them to observe all that I commanded you. My Father is glorified by this that you bear much fruit, and so prove to be My disciples.

The fruit bearing is what God is after. Tares produce no fruits. The filed is fruitless, only that which He had sown in it contains the expected harvest of bread, even the bread of life. Each grain must be multiplied, some 100 others 200 and even 300 fold.

The child within you perhaps went to sleep and the external person took preeminence. While handling people, life's circumstances and troublesome situations we keep on thickening the "spiritual skin" and this results is only sporadic experiences with God's love; hearing His, voice, which requires obedience. Feeling His love takes a childlike state of being, but, as already said, that child within had perhaps fallen asleep.

If you find any value in what I say and you desire closeness of your Father then you must first realize what has happened with your spiritual person within the fleshly shell.

God's eyes scan the world looking for a soul that pleases Him. Are you one of them? He scans the world in order to find His sons and daughters, one must be spiritually alert in order to first discover it and then nurture it.

Motives are extremely important. If your motive is to trumpet out your experiences with God then He had not even spoken to you. If you want to make someone jealous of your spirituality then you have not heard from God. You remain yet an unconverted adult.

Once in one of my meetings a little girl asked her mummy to tell her who were those two beautiful tall man standing behind the preacher. The mother was puzzled for she could not see what her daughter saw so she could not explain. But she brought her girl to me and I told her the truth, "these are my guardian angels."

I only write about it to teach and to make disciples. I share it because the Father loves you. He seeks an audience with you on one-to-one basis. That relationship is not a gift. It is developed over some time for the end-price is not an advertisement, but intimacy; it's secret and hidden from sight.

The Father seeks that child within you. He wants to be needed. He does not seek the self-sustained adult, but rather a helpless child. Providing just for the flesh and treating it as that's all you need, has nothing to do with the Father for that is added to you anyway. The priority is of a quite different quality. Make yourself helpless and hollow before Him. The conversion into a child state of being you must do but all on your own. No one can lay hands on you and give you a powerful life-changing prophecy saying, "For thus sayeth the Lord Thou shalt be like a child."

Look at babies; in both the animal kingdom as well the human they are so cuddly and cute. Even cubs of the ferocious lions are cuddly and delightful. Now, imagine how the Maker of it all looks at us. Does He see the self-sufficient adult or His baby? I think that it is worth every effort to begin the work of conversion into a child-like state of being right now.

A prayer example: "Oh Lord I humble the pride of life and like a child want to depend on you in everything. I will not try to be in control of anything for you are my Father and my Provider. I will not play games nor use double talk. I will not be cynical or overly cautious, I will not exploit any situation to my advantage. I will not be selfish and self-serving. I am the light of the world I will not direct it only to myself, or to my own, but even to my enemies. I return to my innocence, and simple trust. I will practice it each day until I break through to You my Father."

After a while you will be amazed seeing what you have accomplished. You will notice profound changes in your relationship with the Father.

The Bethesda man perhaps for the very first time turned his eyes toward a man instead of the water. After 38 years of studying the movement of water he started to "study" the Way, the Truth and the Life.

NOTE: Thorough excavations of the Poll of Bethesda area in Jerusalem revealed astounding facts. Above the Poll of Bethesda the Romans build huge cisterns, which collected the rainwater during winter. Winters can be quite cold at that elevation, so it is quite difficult to imagine that anyone would have bathed in that pool then. From time to time those cisterns were emptied. The water rushed down to the Bethesda poll along with reddish sediment. Poor and ignorant folk were told that it was an angel stirring the waters. Since sick people could not enter the temple mount they were kept at Bethesda.

With his pallet he went around parading his miracle, but not too many had known that he was the same lame man laying there by the pool, nor did they cared to know for how long he had suffered.

Everyone is on their own trip "studying only the tips of their own noses." The Pharisees rebuked him for violating the Sabbath, but the man said that the one who made him well had told him to 'take his pallet and walk'. And instead of investigating the miracle and the state in which the man was found; and how he was healed, they wanted to know the name of the man who in their eyes violated the Sabbath.

Jesus met him again and told him to 'not sin, lest something worse might happen to him'. From this we learn that the man's illness was caused by sin; and so that nothing worse might happen. The man permitted sin in his life and sin is the way of pain (Ps. 139:24). We also conclude that he, all on his own, had the power to not sin. Just as we can convert ourselves and become like children so the lame man was able to stop sinning. But what was the price? In his case the price was either to sin and be bound up with even a worse bondage, or to not sin and enjoy true freedom.

Once you find pleasure in communing with the Father all other things naturally fall off. The deeper you go into the intimacy with the Father the further you drift away from sin. Your parting with sin should not be painful, for sin is the way of pain. So, part with it today. I have already.

Children are loved and they should never be offended. When they grow up they step on the way of pain for they have been hurt and they look out for any potential culprit. Teenagers go through a rebellious stage because they are confused. Partially they are still kids and partially adults. Now that they have to face the consequences of adulthood it is hard for them to part with childhood. Out of frustration with the status quo teenagers target their parents; all of a sudden they are imperfect, cold and insensitive. They begin to miss the warmth of love encoded in their subconscious mind when they were hugged, bathed and kissed goodnight. Yes, they miss it, but dare not to voice it lest they might come across as still being but children.

The parting with childhood is almost like burial.

Parents have difficulties treating their teenagers as babies; like bathing them and telling them a goodnight story; it's just inappropriate. Thank God that with Him we do not have to go through this process. God is Spirit and so are we. We just have to be taught this and reminded of. In His eyes we are His children no matter what age. No adolescence. He is timeless and heaven is timeless; no one goes through puberty in heaven; no gray hair and no death.

Back to the now healed Bethesda man. After he had learned who was the man that healed him, he then reported it to the Pharisees who again did not care neither about the miracle nor about the man himself, but only about their own doctrines. They had a following, we can say, their own church, and since they were not as anointed as Jesus was, they had much to lose. Not much has changed since. When someone controls something, one takes every single "threat" seriously. These are the fleshly adults, religious business people. When one controls nothing one is happy. Children control nothing and they are happy.

As a child, I remember how I was trying to visualize the future away from home and the care of my parents. I remember a 'conversation' I had with myself. It was a very cold winter. I was sitting by the beaming-with-heat stove.

The wind was hauling and making its own melodies as if trying to get inside and steal the radiance of my fire. "Will I be taken care of?" "Will it be hard to earn a living and get wages? Will I still enjoy God's presence as I do right now? Or, will I struggle in life just as the two of my brothers repeatedly told me hanging over me like vultures 'prophesying' that I won't make it in life? - What do you say Lord?"

Time elapsed and I started to learn my way around the way of pain so many accepted as a given. Curses made no sense to me, neither the 'original sin' theory. My oldest brother looked at my other brother's life and mine and said. "It seems as you are doing well, better then your brothers. What's your secret?"

Peace was my comfort and the inner joy. I could see that His love will never leave me. I am almost 60 and I am still His child. I still sit by the fire listening to the freezing hauling wind recalling the conversation I had with the Lord, or with myself. I was too young to know which was which. I did not know His word well yet. Like the little boy Samuel, who did not distinguish voices, so I was not yet there with the same. But now I know the difference. I still depend on Him for my health and provisions. He takes care of us each day. The greater your mission in life the more of God's love you need. His love sustains me and not my faith, which is never mine.

Raising children and providing for them can be hard, but without the essence of God's love, freely flowing in and out of you can be indeed quite hard. But it does not have to be so. One must only be taught and gently spoken to. One must be loved and then experience His graciousness.

One must learn to let go and not clutch that illusion we call possession, for while still clutching your possessions you will breathe your last. We possess nothing and therefore control nothing. Like children we must willfully and decidedly choose to depend on our Maker in everything. I guarantee you that you will experience His love in your life; even your aging may be reversed. It is all up to Him. I love this state of mind.

More of His love equates life and the less of His love equates death. The fruits of death are: possession, control, suspicions, insecurity and therefore every possible act of grabbing anything that might look like security. Only human bodies are insecure, never our spirit. Vengefulness and self-righteousness, any superiority complex and self-glorification, jealousy and envy; these remain because of the extreme self-valuations. These seal us with death. But what seals us with life? The works of life are as follows: forgiveness for being wronged, arresting envy, jealousy, and covetousness. The letting go of the gratification feeling of possessing something contains a great secret.

Gratefulness for the honor of being chosen as God's steward can replace possessiveness. He has entrusted to us immense treasures to be paid attention to, examined and brought forth in fruitfulness.

Perfect love casts out *all*, and I mean, *ALL* fear; it cannot be otherwise although the "all" is not used in text (1John 4:18, NASB). 'Those that fear are not yet perfected in love' Apostle John said. The seal of truth is the seal of life. Cleaving to the Lord and His ways at all cost. Never accept the status quo. Never yield to any external pressure and the control of man. Don't be ordinary and common, but special in the eyes of God. Once that is established you will see yourself as He sees you. And once you see yourself through His eyes you will look at others with the ever-increasing compassion.

In respect to anyone being your enemy there will come a time that you will become completely blind in this regard; for you will see no enemy; you will not see anyone from your own point of view, but God's. He has no enemies.

The one who is without beginning and no end; the one who created everything for His own pleasure. He does not need to fight for sovereignty, nor fight for control over His own kingdom. Let Him also derive pleasure from your life.

[Jeremiah 15:19] And if **you extract the precious from the worthless**, you will become **My spokesman** (in Hebrew **'My mouth'**).

Will you go for it? Will you embrace it? Will you desire it? Will you discipline yourself? The other alternative is to be as common as the dust of the earth and perish like the masses do. If you believe that you will die like everyone else and even that you must die, then perhaps these words are not for you; so you are permitted to hold on to your beliefs and run with them until the grave. Even if you do eventually die then what's wrong with learning about immortality laws? It is not your believing that changes anything, but the of knowledge.

We have been so indoctrinated to believe that this pressure creates a downright fear of failure. Then with those failures come guilt; and with guilt sadness, and then zip... there went my faith. What your Creator has in store for you is fabulous. So keep on discovering it. I was sent to you to give you those ideas; and perhaps open your eyes to these possibilities. I was sent to the living or rather to make the dead alive in Christ. I was not sent to waste time and throw precious pearls before those that do not value those pearls as precious. There is nothing to agree or disagree with, what's written and what's not written. No false or false theology; no piously and rightly dividing the word of truth preaching the 'sound' or 'silent' doctrine. For God's sake, we are open-minded children!

Listen, even if you grow old and then fall asleep, at least you have enjoyed a fuller life with the living God. Go ahead. Be scripturally correct.

[Hebrews 9:27] And inasmuch as it is appointed for men to die once and after this comes judgment.

But there is another verse where Jesus declared; [John 8:51] truly, truly, I say to you, if anyone keeps My word he will never see death.

Which verse is better? Freedom! It is all up to you my dear friend. If you hesitate to embrace it means then perhaps you've been hurt or disappointed and are afraid to repeat that experience. Perhaps, you were taught to have an absolute faith and while presuming of having that faith, in your presumption, you have made many blunders.

You have promised to not let yourself be misled again, for so you have judged even those that taught you faith. Through this prejudice you keep out a watch for any 'false prophets and teachers' lest they might disappoint you again.

Someone wrote to me telling me that I have said, "Everything will be okay." "But it is not okay" the reply was, blaming me for even saying such words. There are so many unstable people. Others imagine that my prayers have some magical powers, so when someone dies I am guilty. So many are mentally ill and they seek help from anyone showing any signs of compassion, and once they find one they become obsessive and possessive to the point of supposing that the preacher was sent only for them. They try to wrap him up around their own finger. In the same way I cannot tell you when the rapture would occur during your lifetime, for even Jesus Himself does not know that, but only the Father.

[Matthew 24:36] "But of that day and hour no one knows, not even the angels of heaven, nor the Son, but the Father alone."

This verse alone trashes any doctrines of those that propagate a belief that God has no son, for Jesus is the Father. Yet, in so many words Jesus said that WE would come and make OUR abode with you. Some theology cannot be blindly accepted and followed as a fixed doctrine; it must be understood according to the explanation of the Holy Spirit.

[John 14:23] If anyone loves Me, he will keep My word; and My Father will love him, and We will come to him and make Our abode with him.

Jesus clearly states here that He will love you, His Father will love you, and THEY will make THEIR abode with you. These words cannot be ritualized. Again, they must be understood. This spiritual grasp can only come to those who have detached their minds from their egos. And yes, it comes when certain conditions are met. The more hollow you become the more can fill your being. "The more shallow the hollow the more of God and His essence of love."

Your progress is very individual and private, and nobody can interfere with it. I cannot give you a prophecy as to your own future and guarantee you immortality and if I did I would be but a false prophet. I would base that promise on my faith for you; yet God did not give me that gift of faith for you. And if you are dead then you cannot testify against me. But perhaps you have left your testimony to those with hammer and nail in hand; ready to shut your casket down and lay hands on your money. Now they blabber out their 'proof'. This no-dying business is very dangerous, for the field and tares don't nor ever will get it. Unless they find in themselves God's seed and cling to it they will perish like everyone else. Faith without works is already dead before one dies.

Mental faith comes from the Greek type philosophical mind. Some cling to Paul, while others to James in this regard. The closest to Jesus was James (Jacob) for he was the Lord's own brother. However, both are right because Paul talks about being saved, and James speaks about proving the fruit of salvation with the works/fruits of faith.

When we are self-critical and humble ourselves then no life's circumstances must humble us. When we walk in that humility we receive His sight and see ourselves in His light.

Once in Nepal, Jesus visited a young missionary brother and told him that on a certain day He would take him. This brother told his wife about it. One day several missionaries gathered to pray. While they were still praying the man disappeared leaving only his shoes on the floor. Jesus took him just as He Himself appeared and disappeared after His resurrection so He did for this brother. This testimony I received from eyewitnesses.

The Holy Spirit transported Philip from place to place. It is in the Bible and it is the absolute truth, why so many do not believe that it really was so is because they are still ordinary and they like to stay that way. Belonging to masses means that I must perish like the masses.

What about the chosen nation, royal priesthood (1Peter 2:9)? But you are not the field my dear friend, you are not the tare; you are His good seed, which He Himself had sown in the filed. Who are you really, do you know?

No matter how we look at it we are the salt of this earth, the light and God's high standard. You will, and even must bear much fruit for that fruit makes you glorious. God takes only the glorious people, the overcomers and the fruit bearers, not the dust. Dust He spits out of His mouth. He seeks to fellowship with those who like Jesus take the challenge and overcome.

* * *

Chapter 11

ENDLESS LOVE

Perhaps I have raised the bar too high and you are convinced that you can't jump that high. My dear friend it is not my bar, but His. He is the Truth and He tells the truth. He knows you better than you do.

God's love for you has no end. If you ask Him 'why do you love me?' He would have answered, "I love you because I love you." The "because" is the point upon which God's ways hang.

[Exodus 33:19] "...I will be gracious to whom I will be gracious, and will show compassion on whom I will show compassion."

Also, God's choices are irrevocable, just as His anointings (choices) and callings are unchangeable (Romans 11:29). God cannot deny Himself or change His choice for these are eternal made by the Eternal One.

God can only change a punishment when someone repents, which means: He will change adversities into blessings when someone is willing to change and calls to Him.

This also is very clear and 100% certain, God works with us and amongst us. How we treat others and ourselves determines the outcome. He made us all and like a parent He holds the ownership right. Although God gave us the free will, that free will is only for the earth because of our physical bodies, but it ends being free and independent the moment a body dies.

On the other side the free will loses any meaning and any affect. God's ultimate and sovereign ways overrule everything. He is completely sovereign and completely mighty and no matter how you might want to change it with your theology or common beliefs, the fact remains the same. He tolerates a lot of our inanities because we are still growing and learning. You can't fight with the Almighty. He can give you time to play, and let you fall and the grace to get up again.

Someone said to me, "Without your teaching I could never come up with the ideas I have come up with and invented something that made me rich." This now very rich man said to me that my teaching set him on a course of becoming a millionaire. I have created in him straight and logical thinking. Once he was even my friend, but that was only one-sided. He was feeding on my knowledge; you can say that he was smart, but was he really? Well, it depends on how you look at things. If you look at things from the money point of view than yes, but when from God's point of view then no. Why? Because he had produced no good fruit and showed only the negative fruit of selfishness. The Holy Spirit was grieved and I was too. Time is ticking and what you sow one day you will have to reap. In a short run you gain, but in long run you lose. When I asked him if he could sponsor our orphanage in India and donate some of his money; his response was this: "Joseph you will never be rich." Then he changed the subject and gave not one red cent.

Opportunity knocks on some doors, and these opportunities are too often exchanged for the temporary matter, which rusts and moths eat.

I left dejected and very disappointed with this proud millionaire who just thanked me for my teachings.

I came in the name of the Lord with wisdom from on high, but so many have just taken what they wanted and then spit me out. It's not nice to say it, but it is my experience and the fact of my life. And just BECAUSE he said these words to me the Lord had visited me that night and told me what will happen later on in my life: "Although you do not seek wealth, just because he said this to you I will give you wealth he only can dream about."

I humble myself to the level of a child and act like a child, that I might enter the kingdom and I have entered it long time ago. But these child-like ways of mine fools many into believing that I am naive and prime target open for manipulations; and although I let them go their own way, yet one day God will slip them the bill. I wash my hands off them and move on leaving any repayment to the Most High.

[Psalms 105:15] Do not touch My anointed ones, and do My prophets no harm.

Once God chooses you; and is gracious to you; and loves you, then you know it 100% that you are His. There is no guessing in this. It's a fact and anyone competing with you will lose.

The truth must come not from any teaching, but from the Father Himself. However you may go about it, the stream of His love toward you must come from above and never from below, not even from the Bible, or faith, or claiming, but directly from the Father.

God the Spirit, the Holy Spirit cannot be constantly among us for most of the time He is grieved.

He comes because of His anointed. Always. The anointed has the power to bring Him closer to you or to shield Him from the unworthy. When someone acts in pride, jealousy and tries to compete with God's anointed, one does not only grieve the Lord, but can also become even as His enemy. Sooner or later judgment will fall.

Now, the question of a belief comes to the fore. Some would say, "We do not believe that." Okay. Don't. Contrary to any former teachings, your faith makes no difference, because your faith changes nothing in the realm of the Spirit. Your faith is inactive until the gift of faith is given, and when it is released, it is only for salvation.

The faith of which Jesus spoke was the Father's gift that they might believe in His Son the Messiah; and to not repeat myself to often, that faith made them whole. Salvation embraces not only our soul or spirit but also our bodies. Healing is the integral part of salvation. This information does not condemn you for lacking faith. It is so. Period.

[Deuteronomy 23:14] "Since the LORD your God walks in the midst of your camp to deliver you **and to defeat your enemies before you**, therefore your camp must be holy; and **He must not see anything indecent among you or He will turn away from you.**

Today, the Holy Spirit, which came to us on the day of Pentecost, does the same. If the enemy is you then God will turn on you, yet He comes to defeat those that come against His anointed.

He is the Perfect Love that dispels all fear, but puts fear on your enemies. For you, He casts out fears while for them He creates dreadful and paralyzing dread. Do you understand the Covenant-keeping and Loving God?

God is not some 'syrupy lovey lollypop pappy'. He is God, which an average believer knows little about.

When someone wants to come closer, even into His awesome presence, one must know Him and His ways. Just as one comes in the presence of a king one must be prepared and use special etiquette.

* * *

Chapter 15

GOD'S LOVE FOR HIS CHOSEN

[Jeremiah 30:17] 'For I will restore you to health and I will heal you of your wounds,' declares the LORD, 'because they have called you an outcast, saying: "It is Zion; no one cares for her."'

Those that still propagate this sort of a replacement theology know nothing about God's covenantal love. These are the goats, which shall stand ashamed on the left side, while the sheep (not lovers of self, but also of God's chosen people) on the right.

Once a man came to me with a roll of paper on which he printed all the verses that speak of God's (temporary) rejection of His people. This man singled out all negativities and avoided all verses that speak of God's love and restoration. I pointed to him the end promises, restoration and God's everlasting love.

If the Eternal God who bases His covenant on His faithfulness changes His mind; then perhaps He might also change His mind about that malicious man?

I showed him many scriptures, which I will bring here just to show God's love for us all, for He chooses a people through whom He draws other peoples to Himself.

The bitter sour-faced man showed but displeasure. He did not want to share what he believed he had. His heart was beating but only for himself.

He knew very little that a cultivated selfishness is going to implode. Eventually, anything self-serving will curl upon itself and implode. That's the law. But he knew nothing about God's laws, just as many who have cultivated an aversion to the law don't know.

God said, "I will restore your fortunes. I will heal you. I will bless you and do better for you at the end than in the beginning" and that is His love for Israel forever.

I say that this man was sick in his soul. Who in the right mind would take the time weeding out all the negative verses in the Bible and then hurl them at the Jew, bluntly telling him or her that 'you are rejected forever. 'I have read it in your own book which your people wrote'... Also the church seems to be afflicted with this strange malady, which is jealousy and bitter envy. Antagonism against the Jew started when Christianity appropriated the Jewish Bible.

[Ezekiel 36:6-12] 'Therefore prophesy concerning the land of Israel and say to the mountains and to the hills, to the ravines and to the valleys, "Thus says the Lord GOD, 'Behold, I have spoken in My jealousy and in My wrath.'"

Yes, God was angry at Israel because Israel was far from being perfect. God's love for Israel is intense and unquenchable and to understand it one must taste at least a tiny bit of it. But then God looks at the nations what they have done to His beloved and fires back:

[6] **'But because you have endured the insults of the nations.'** "Therefore thus says the Lord GOD, 'I have sworn that surely the nations which are around you will themselves endure their insults.

God has not changed, for He remains the same yesterday, today and forever. Only His treatment of anything set in time does change.

He cannot change His nature in the New Testament or in Christianity for that matter. The only thing that has changed is that 2000 years ago His firstborn, special and unique Son appeared, died and rose from the dead. Then went back to the Father triumphant asking for the gift of the Holy Spirit, and thus He became our intercessor. He intercedes for us, which does not mean that we must dump on him our sin, unrighteousness, and keep Him busy shielding us from God's wrath.

But you, O mountains of Israel, you will put forth your branches and bear your fruit for My people Israel; for they will soon come. For, behold, I am for you, and I will turn to you, and you will be cultivated and sown. I will multiply men on you, all the house of Israel, all of it; and the cities will be inhabited and the waste places will be rebuilt. I will multiply on you man and beast; and they will **increase** and be **fruitful**; and I will cause you to be inhabited as you were formerly and **will treat you better than at the first.**

God can't wait to bless you, forget the past and create everything new and fresh. He practically can't wait to show you His everlasting and fervent love. Oh what a great Father we have. His ways are wonderful. He can't wait to heal you, restore your youth and make you eternal like He is Himself.

The knowledge of the Lord is wonderful. "Just because others insulted you they have insulted Me," He said. And, "while I prosper you they will cringe in their jealousies and envies and will not be willing to admit their error." They will accuses you, that's your cross to which you nail your weaknesses. But after the cross comes resurrection.

[11] "Thus you will know that I am the LORD. 'Yes, I will cause men—My people Israel—to walk on you and possess you, so that you will become their inheritance **and never again bereave them of children.'"**

It is the common anti-Semitism, which blames the Jew for every trouble in the world. With that malice and prejudice comes the jealousy of the Jewish gold, Jewish prowess and envy of high positions in banking, film and media industry.

An anchorman on the CNN network dared to express such anti-Semitic views and lost his show. Even gentiles can any longer endure such insults for God has turned their hearts toward His people to bless them.

[13-15] Thus says the Lord GOD, "**Because they say to you**, you are a devourer of men and have bereaved your nation of children, therefore you will no longer devour men and no longer bereave your nation of children," declares the Lord GOD. "I will not let you hear insults from the nations anymore, nor will you bear disgrace from the peoples any longer, nor will you cause your nation to stumble any longer," declares the Lord GOD."

In this day and age those that curse Israel only curse themselves, for it is a time of God's complete restoration. The Bible is clear.

[9] 'For, behold, I am for you, and I will turn to you, and you will be cultivated and sown.

How can anyone not recognize it and be present-minded. It is like those in the South today (USA) yearning for the free Negro labor in the name of white supremacy.

For hundreds of years now slavery has been abolished and yet the prejudice and hatred toward the Afro-Americans still exists. The unwillingness to change is a goat-like.

I do not conform but only to the Truth. God hates slavery of any form for this reason He raised up liberators from Moses to Jesus and even myself today. Freedom is misconstrued because true freedom cannot be taken advantage of. I am free and want the same for you. I do not indoctrinate.

As you keep on reading this chapter till the end you will realize that the goats represent the unloving while the sheep the loving. People of different races test other peoples and in the same way God tests you and the church regarding the Jewish people and the Nation of Israel. But all racists have one huge virus in them; they hate the Jews and all other races; accept themselves.

[Matthew 25:32] All the nations will be gathered before Him; and He will separate them from one another, as the shepherd separates the sheep from the goats; and He will put the sheep on His right, and the goats on the left.

Self-love only blocks many from experiencing God's unadulterated love. Unless they part with those prejudices they will only hear the gospel for the witness and then comes the final judgment.

A seed can turn into a tare for both have God's life. Cain was also God's seed like Abel and Seth, but Cain chose to be the tare. God gave him over to his OWN ways.

God did not create tares; they came to be through a rebellious act of Cain; so he became the possessor of just the temporary and dead matter and created fictional values. With these illusory values Cain infected the world causing wars. Today, people kill over a bank's promissory notes, which inflation can quickly erase. In 1930s the Deutsche Mark was losing value by seconds. Wheelbarrows were too small to carry all the banknotes with which to buy a loaf of bread. Hitler came to power by riding on this bad economic news. Prices of the daily commodities had reached billions. The bank paper was practically worthless. Hitler blamed communists for it and the Jews who provided the ideology of Karl Marks. Hundreds of years before Hitler, Martin Luther had sown those seeds of prejudice and hatred. With Luther's words Hitler fuelled the racist propaganda also amongst Christians.

What shall we Christians do with this damned, **rejected** race of Jews? Their synagogues and schools should be burnt... their homes destroyed... their prayer books, Talmuds and their holy books taken away. The rabbis should be forbidden to teach under penalty of death... Traveling privileges should be revoked... The Jews should not be allowed to gain interest from their loans... To the young and old, both man and women the flail, the axe, the hoe, the distaff and spindle should be given and let them earn their bread with the sweat of their noses..."

("Martin Luther, January 4, 1543, quotation taken from "Martin Luther, Life and Works 1522 to 1546," GTB Siebenstern 412, 1977, page 275.)

Although Christianity was born in Judaism and in the land of Israel time has warped the mindset of many Christians.

God is Spirit. He dwells in a timeless realm. He changes not. His eternal covenant with Israel, which is based on His character rather than ours, is everlasting; hence, timeless.

Luther whose major achievement was the translation of Paul's Letter to the Romans spiked it with his own ideas. Yet, how can one change the clear message of the apostle directed to the non-Jewish Romans, especially chapters 9 through 11? There must have been some kind of blindness on Luther; and judging from his actions and words we see this,

[John 5:42] but I know you, that you do not have the love of God in yourselves.

Luther seemed to have the pharisaic pride; they were prideful and spiteful and Luther justified himself with the same but against the Jews. He viewed all Jews as the Pharisees.

Luther, as a result did not know whom he was worshipping and his salvation by grace was incomplete due to his exclusion of the Jewish people. Luther missed this verse,

[John 4:22] You worship what you do not know; we worship what we know, for salvation is from the Jews.

If you single out Jesus out of the entire Jewish body then your salvation may not be complete. And as shocking as that may sound, it is not I who said, but Jesus.
This love for Israel is not natural my friend. It is God's love, which is never selfish. A narcissistic love is but a fleshly love, which is no love at all; and many believers play with it.

[Romans 9:1-4; 12:1-2] I am telling the truth in Christ, I am not lying, my conscience testifies with me in the Holy Spirit, that I have great sorrow and unceasing grief in my heart. **For I could wish that I myself were accursed, separated from Christ for the sake of my brethren, my kinsmen according to the flesh, who are Israelites**, to whom belongs the adoption as sons. (...) I say then, God has not rejected His people, has He? May it never be! (...) God has not rejected His people whom He foreknew.

It is quite clear, for Paul speaks plainly and hardly in complicated riddles. **God has never rejected His own people.**
Had God rejected His people then He would have to reject Himself too. God, in a whim of temper might also reject those saved by grace today, those who go to church to hear the message of the blessed assurance. God changes not. Without the Jew we would not have the Bible for they preserved it through the ages. Without the twelve tribes of Israel we would not have the Northern kingdom Israel, with Jeroboam the son of Nebat, Ahab and Jezebel, Elijah and Elisha. We would not have the Lost Sheep of the House of Israel today.

[Romans 11:25)] For I do not want you, brethren, to be ignorant regarding this mystery—so that you will not be wise in your own estimation—that **a partial hardening** has happened to Israel **until the fullness of the Gentiles has come in.**

Obviously God has only suspended Israel in a partial unbelief. Just as faith is God's gift; and—for reasons only known to God—He can also harden any heart, yes even yours and mine; and make anyone spiritually blind with unbelief. He is the ALL Mighty God and not a part-mighty god.

This partial unbelief **God gave** to Israel (Romans 11:8) for a reason and that reason and drive is love. "God so loved the world... (John 3:16)." You are the *whoever*.

Not all will believe after hearing (Romans 10:14 &17) do they? First must come an anointed preacher with words and sounds. Then God's gift of faith is also released. Anyone who made provision and became a receptacle for that faith is accepted, saved, even born again.

So, God stopped the preaching of the Gospel to the Jews and forced Peter and Paul to preach it to the Gentiles and they rejoiced for they had been waiting for it. How would they hear without a preacher?

[Acts 13:46-47]...behold, we are turning to the Gentiles. "For so the Lord has commanded us, 'I HAVE PLACED YOU AS A LIGHT FOR THE GENTILES, THAT YOU MAY BRING SALVATION TO THE END OF THE EARTH.'"

[Romans 11:12-16] Now if their (Israel's) transgression is riches for the world and their failure is riches for the Gentiles, how much more will their fulfillment be!

Here Paul address the non-Jews. "**But I am speaking to you who are Gentiles.** Inasmuch then as I am an apostle of Gentiles..."

Clearly, the rejection and temporary suspension if Israel is for the sake of the world, which the world took and hurled at the Jew, just as some still do today in the church.

God is sovereign and omniscient because time does not play any role to Him. He sees the entire history of mankind in a split second. His love is much greater than we have ever imagined. So Paul, being saturated with God's love, continues.

"For if their rejection is the reconciliation of the world, what will their acceptance be but life from the dead? If the first piece of dough is holy, (Natural Israel) the lump is also (Christians); and if the root is holy (Israel), the branches (Gentile Christians) are too."

Why do things have to be so complicated and why must we search things out; use deduction and logic and repeatedly keep on "turning that 'chicken' over the fire?" The answer is clear, we have complicated ourselves on purpose and out of straight ways we made bundles of threads and knots making the job of untying even harder. However, the very work of untying is a sign of God's love for you for He is reaching out to you even right now making you understand that things don't have to be so complicated.

In the entire world, the most complicated theology comes from the German-speaking regions.

His yoke is easy. His burden is light and His ways are straight. There would be no need for the five-fold-ministries if we were converted into a child-like state of mind and being. We have become so sophisticated and so important in our own eyes that we have blinded ourselves to simple and straightforward truths. 'We go in rapture. Jews suffer some more. We are so special because God gave us grace...'

The same God who loves Israel with great passion reaches out to you right now and says to you, "I am your God and your Father." If He loves Israel and you love His people then you begin to bathe in His love. If you do not care about His love for those He chose to write and preserve the Bible with their own lives for you; then you bathe in someone else's bath, but it is not God's.

No matter how you may feel regarding Israel, you must look at it all through the apple of God's eye (Zechariah 2:9).

Look how great is God's love for you. Those who wrote the Bible spoke about themselves not with self-love, but critically. How many can afford to speak of themselves in this fashion? Hence, the Bible is the True Word of God.

Without the Bible we would not have anti-Semitism, Catholicism nor Reformation, Luther's spiteful words, Hitler and Auschwitz. You can 'blame' it all on the Bible and its authors, but unfortunately God has determined that only the remnant shall be saved (Jer. 31:7 & Rom. 9:27). And that remnant is His seed that will be stored in the heavenly barn. That seed is known as something eatable from which bread can be baked. It also speaks of the Bread of Life that came down from heaven in God's chosen package (John 4:22). You may not like this Jewish package, but that is beside the point.

[2Samuel 22:26-28 & Psalms 18:25-27] With the kind You show Yourself kind, with the blameless You show Yourself blameless; with the pure You show Yourself pure, and with the perverted You show Yourself astute. And You save an afflicted people; but Your eyes are on the haughty whom You abase.

God does not choose good people for bad people. He seeks prodigal sons and daughters that is His objective. Once He finds them by then all the rest will have finished their mission on earth. So find out who you are.

***

Chapter 16

GOD'S LOVE & HELL

Cain left God's presence and went his way doing his 'own' thing. Cain had been excluded from the life of God; he has nothing to look forward to. Cain's mission on earth is terminated at the point of death. A tare that is burned up, which means permanently annihilated, in both the physical and spiritual realms. Such in God's mind has never existed. Such have no recollection of anything because they are not in timeless heaven. Likewise Judas the son of perdition will be no more. The word "perdition" Jesus used. In Greek it means a complete loss or annihilation. Tell God that He is unfair. Judas can't object, having no recollection or any awareness of ever existing. That is the super righteousness of God and yes, His love. Do you see that we tend to place our humanism and fairness in the wrong place? I wonder what causes it? When it matters we are silent, but when it does not, we protest. Besides being ignorant we also lack the love of God within ourselves.

Today the study of human DNA has exhibited many hidden mysteries. We are living in an astounding age. We know that our genes remember for in distant past they had been stamped with something. Through the chromosome 'Y' we can trace and determine your ancestral lineage. This maze of wants, desires, animosities, affections, predispositions, abilities and disabilities reside in us all. We fall prey to the ancestral whims within us or we rule over them something brand new.

Generally people do not like to change while worshipping the good old days. Reformation is out of the question. Anything new is met with suspicion and resistance. The process is so slow that by the time you grasp one fragment; another gene in you makes you cling to something old and well established, saying, "why rocking the boat?"

Yes, we resist change, but we like the new electronic gadgets, cellphones, and new cars and better new convinces.

[Ephesians 4:17-19] So this I say, and affirm together with the Lord, that **you walk no longer** just as the Gentiles also walk, in the futility of their mind. Being darkened in their understanding, excluded from the life of God because of the ignorance that is in them, because of the hardness of their heart. And they **having become callous** have given themselves over to sensuality for the practice of every kind of impurity with greediness.

Obviously Paul was bringing something very new. He tried to change the Gentiles telling them to NO LONGER walk in the former manner but new.

[Romans 1:24-28] Therefore God gave them over in the lusts of their hearts to impurity, so that their bodies would be dishonored among them. (...) For this reason God gave them over to degrading passions; for their women exchanged the natural function for that which is unnatural. And in the same way also the men abandoned the natural function of the woman and burned in their desire toward one another, men with men committing indecent acts and receiving in their own persons the due penalty of their error. And just as they did not see fit to acknowledge God any longer, God gave them over to a depraved mind, to do those things, which are not proper.

These strong words portray the power of our will. When we repeatedly give ourselves over to flesh, flesh we shall have.

I have nothing against homosexuals and lesbians. I pity them, their ways and their chosen lifestyle. They will not burn in hell forever. They will not enter into the kingdom of heaven; they have no eternal life. They will not exist on either side because eventually they are given over to what the really want, love and worship—flesh. Once the giving over happens repentance is impossible. These are not my words.

Many do not believe in the eternal afterlife because it is not given to them to believe. The attachment to just the fleshly pleasures completely blinds and blocks them from believing. Those who go to church, do that just in case there is life after death. This is their state of confusion. The scripture is clear about it. Such were some before, but are no longer immoral or unrighteous.

[1Corinthians 6:9-11] Or do you not know that the unrighteous will not inherit the kingdom of God? Do not be deceived; neither fornicators, nor idolaters, nor adulterers, nor effeminate, nor homosexuals, nor thieves, nor the covetous, nor drunkards, nor revilers, nor swindlers, will inherit the kingdom of God. Such were some of you; but you were washed, but you were sanctified, but you were justified in the name of the Lord Jesus Christ and in the Spirit of our God.

That means that they were not given over. They repented and turned to Christ. The blood of Jesus cleansed them from all sin and they will enjoy eternity with Him.

[Hebrews 6:4-8] For in the case of those who have once been enlightened and have tasted of the heavenly gift and have been made partakers of the Holy Spirit, and have tasted the good word of God and the powers of the age to come, and then have fallen away, **it is impossible to renew them again to repentance**, since they again crucify to themselves the Son of God and put Him to open shame. For ground that drinks the rain, which often falls on it and brings forth vegetation useful to those for whose sake it is also tilled, receives a blessing from God. But if it yields thorns and thistles, it is worthless and close to being cursed, and it ends up being burned.

It also means that some were once homosexual, or gay as it is the modern term for both men and women, but are gay no more. The possibility to change is there. But if anyone says that one cannot change anymore, then that is a clear sign of being given over to a god of one's own flesh. The love of just the physical pleasure on this side seals one with just the physical. They have glorified their flesh and its passions as if there is nothing more in life than that. Those who practice any form of immorality and repeatedly fall in love with it; are either already given over to it, or are about to be given over when their cup of immorality becomes full. Just as Cain could not return anymore to God and was given over to his own ways, so it can be with everyone that disregards even this time of grace and the outreach of His love.

God is not the monster who created hell, but rather man. Jesus only alluded to this monstrosity in one of His parables about the poor man Lazarus and the rich man. Religion gave us hell and spiked the Bible with references to it. Sheol (Hebrew) is not hell. Hades (Greek) is not hell, but both words refer to a place of the sleeping dead.

Hell would be Gehinnom (Hebrew) from which Gehenna (Greek) emerged. These words denote a place of burning, which was outside Jerusalem in the extension of the Kidron valley. All refuse, idols and anything worn by the lepers was being burned in Gehinnom. The smoke seemed to be perpetual and from this came the idea of hell.

A lake of fire is not hell and in the entire Book of Revelations does not mention Gehenna but Hades, which uniformly is being translated as hell (mainly in KJV). Perhaps the theology of hell was quite successful in recruiting and keeping more of the hell scared followers?

God is not sadistic, nor is He vengeful. We may interpret scripture in this light, but when vengeance is left up to God then the cup of evil gets gradually filled up. An example of this is found Genesis 16:16. God said to Abraham that the 'iniquity of the Amorite is not yet complete.'

Obviously, God never acts on an impulse, but does He have to? What we sow grows until harvest. It is the same with a complete iniquity as well as with righteousness. It's a matter of time.

God said that Abraham's descendants, Israel, would have to go to Egypt, where they would live for 430 years. What was the reason? God also loved the Canaanite peoples and waited for their repentance because He is slow to anger. Hey, God was still after Cain for his descendants established Canaan (Genesis 15: 19). I mention it again to show you an augmented picture of God's love. However, we have not mentioned that God was still seeking Cain and his seed. But none of them returned; otherwise we would also have their lineage in the Bible, but we don't.

God is gracious and grace is space. So He kept His people in Egypt for so long and even longer in the wilderness for 40 years. That's how God out of His love sacrificed Israel for the rest of the world. He does not delight in death of the wicked.

[Ezekiel 18:23] "Do I have any pleasure in the death of the wicked," declares the Lord GOD, "rather than that he should turn from his ways and live?"

Once you come closer to Him and bathe in God's love then from time to time He will whisper into your spirit to check this or that. Sometimes I stopped in the middle of my preaching before hundreds of people. I sent my helper to bring me Concordance; and while people were waiting I was comparing the original text with the translated one. I then confirmed what God's Spirit just whispered to me. I redirected my entire sermon and took a completely different turn. Today, I am thankful for what I did. But those ho could not change with me started to oppose me and many doors shut down on me.

* * *

Chapter 17

GOD'S LOVE & SATAN

God did not create the devil. Man did. God did not create hell. Man did. No matter what anyone's near-death experience might have been, or someone came back from hell and told about it, those things are idiosyncratic.

[Genesis 3: 8] They heard the sound of the LORD God walking in the garden in the cool of the day, and the man and his wife hid themselves from the presence of the LORD God among the trees of the garden.'

God did not create an evil Satan, but angels, which He can use according to any arising need on earth. Any angel can serve God's love or judgment. There are no permanently evil angels, nor permanently good ones, that is a pure human speculation and vain imagination.

God did not make Cain evil, but Cain chose evil. God did not make Adam and Eve sinful nor unrighteous He taught them the difference between good and evil. To this very day we are in the school of God's ways. But instead we mystified Him and His word; and in the process we have complicated ourselves.

Yes, God sent the creature Nechash who became the serpent. An angel spoke through the beast of the field like the angel who spoke through the donkey of Balaam. When God pronounced curses, these were never permanent, but not like those curses the pagans fear and see them as something final. God never doomed anyone, for that was purely Adam's choice when he was unwilling to repent. Yes, repentance was already then provided. The lessons learnt would have turned Adam into a wise man, after his repentance. I know it for a fact.

The picture of God and His kingdom is very plain. His ways are very simple. Yes, they are clear in children's eyes, but complicated in the eyes of the so called mature.

Adam was the head of Eve, and if he had repented his wife would have followed. Their genes would have carried different properties then. You might say that the experiment had failed; and God made a blunder. I don't think so. Remember that He is love and all that He did was for the good of Adam and Eve and for their best. As the all-seeing God He saw the future, and if so then with that repentance was also provided.

Religion twisted this picture by blaming Satan for the 'disaster' and Adam and Eve for not being smart enough for they fell for the supposed temptation.

Nechash only came because God had permitted and even instigated it Himself.

He had a plan for us and to make us even much more like He is Himself. Hence the words of the angel that spoke through (the serpent) Nechash.

[Genesis 3:5] For God knows that in the day you eat from it your eyes will be opened, and you will be like God, knowing good and evil.

What was that good and evil? They were sinless. They felt no physical pain yet, no fear nor had they experienced a sleepless night. Did God want them to stay in such a state? – I don't think so, just as your own children not supposed to stay in diapers. God was preparing them for a life in the entire world and not just in the little Garden of Eden.

God wanted for Adam and Eve to experience pain from which quite naturally they would turn away. He wanted them to see what is right and wrong and then choose the right. That turning away from evil and choosing what is right is being more and more like God. Enoch succeeded in this practice of choices, why no one else could do the same? Failing and blaming is easy, but taking responsibility is being a God-like.

The assumption that there were no other people on earth, but only Adam and Eve, messes up our straight thinking.

Did God want Adam and Eve to inhabit only that one patch of land in Mesopotamia called Eden? Didn't He want them to multiply and replenish the entire earth?

Although for a while Adam and Eve remained in the region called Eden they were not meant to stay there all of their lives. Yes, God planned for them to populate the earth with their kind.

Cain left the Eden region and went to another region called Nod. He is the extreme example of a completely mishandled knowledge of good and evil. Clearly, Cain chose evil thus he greatly grieved his parents, but foremost, God. Now, if he so firmly chose to be evil, even a tare; then the same possibility was available in the opposite direction. Was it not?

God gave us the choice to choose good or evil, hate or love, curse or blessing, life or death, being cold or hot... Choose! That mean we have got the power, but we do not use it; doubting ourselves. God prods to sharpen this power to be aimed at Him. LOVE ME! He says.

[Deuteronomy 30:19-20] So choose life in order that you may live, you and your descendants, by loving the LORD your God...

Jesus said to the lame man, "Sin no more." He also said to the adulterous woman, "Sin no more" and that was still before the cross and resurrection. There was not yet the so-called Pauline gospel for the Gentiles; and yet both the lame man and the adulterous woman were told to not sin anymore. Why did we indoctrinate ourselves that it is impossible to ever part with sin and that without the blood of Jesus it is impossible to not sin? As I have repeatedly stated, sin is the way of pain. The fruit of sin is pain and no one likes pain. So stop sin, which hurts and you will stop all pain.

This may sound like a great discovery, but it isn't. It is as old as the world. Someone muddied up our straight thinking.

God wanted to infuse the populated earth with the seed of righteousness, that's the reason why we have genealogies and the tracing of patrimonial lines in the Bible.

[Romans 9:13] Just as it is written, "Jacob I loved, but Esau I hated."

Esau, like Cain, was given over to his own ways, which were purely fleshly. Esau ridiculed and completely disregarded his spiritual heritage, that's how much he was in love with the physical stuff. The sniffing of the wild game meant more to him than the realm of God who made it all.

We can enjoy the physical world to the fullest and have great fun, but God wants to take part in that joy.

Religion created an idea that to serve God is a drag, even an obligation. Like a doorman standing outside at the church entry snapping his whip; and whoever hears its crack quickly runs inside lest he or she meets the fiery hell.

Doom and gloom, the original sin, fiery hell with grotesque creatures dragging you down to the bottomless pit is what man has invented for their fearful followers. I try to snap you out of this complete nonsense reading the same Bible seeing it in God's light. The time has come to know God's word through God's eyes, not through denominational, sectarian or dogmatic points of view.

Open your eyes and see the light. Open your heart and release the by God deposited in you essence of love. Let it flow back to Him for when it flows back to you it comes with an ever-greater power. Yes, thank Him for what you read here. Thank Him for giving you this book and for crossing our paths. Turn on your gratitude and feel something marvelous inside. Do not compare yourself with me, but rather thank God for His gift.

[Luke 6:35-36] Love your enemies, and do good, and lend, expecting nothing in return; and your reward will be great, and you will be sons of the Most High; for He Himself is kind to ungrateful and evil men. Be merciful, just as your Father is merciful.

You can read this verse through the mind of the "religious paranoia" or intelligently. Should we love our enemies (people) even heal them, but hate the angelic enemy Satan? Are we half-and-half paranoid schizophrenics? What's going on? On one hand we are the sons of light, children of love and while on the other we are vindictive haters. I understand this picture: a wolf is attacking a mother who is clutching her baby. She kicks the wolf while lovingly shielding her baby. If you fight the enemy while protecting others then that's all right, that is called HESID. But if you imagine that wolf being your enemy while the truth is that there is no wolf attacking you at all; then you are out of date. Please update yourself. God did not create Satan so that He could have someone to fight with.

He is Love. He told us so. "Love your enemies, do good to them for such are the sons of the Most High."

If Satan is your malicious enemy, and you like to call him the devil then what about the business of loving your enemy?

Do you know for a fact what Satan has done to you? Can you win your case against the devil in the court of law? Someone gave us this hogwash without any understanding of the Almighty God and His nature. Zoroaster, Pharisees and Mani sought God but also following. Rooted in dualism God did not speak to those men as He did to Abraham or Moses. They just competed just as Muhammad did. Sectarianism and organized religion always excludes an individuum because such is often viewed as a potential threat to the leadership. As history shows such were quickly was labeled a heretic.

* * *

THE HEAVENLY LOVE & PEACE

Do not allow malice and vengeance to rule over your soul. The standard of love is divine. In that love we find perfect peace, security and mighty joy.

[Numbers 6: 24-26] The LORD bless you, and keep you; The LORD make His face shine on you, and be gracious to you; he LORD lift up His countenance on you, and give you peace.

The Kingdom of God is not split into the realm of darkness and light, or into good and evil, but is one; only the physical or visible realm is divided. God's logic is found in the Bible and here is what He gave us.

The opposite of a blessing is a curse. While the Lord blesses you, curses fall on your enemies. Why? – Because you are loving and so you heap burning coals on those that made themselves as your enemy. "The Lord keep you." The opposite of being kept is letting go or giving one over to one's own. In this precarious world one becomes then a lord of his or her (own) life, an illusion with which so many are sealed.

[Romans 12:19-21] Never take your own revenge, beloved, but leave room for the wrath of God, for it is written, "Vengeance is Mine, I will repay," says the Lord. "But if your enemy is hungry, feed him, and if he is thirsty, give him a drink; for in so doing you will **heap burning coals on his head.**" Do not be overcome by evil, but overcome evil with good.

Perhaps it is hard to let go of this kind of an emotion. Long time ago it was hard for me. Today it is easy and I do it all the time. I have practiced and I won over my soul. My renewed mind rules over my soul.

"The Lord makes His face shine on you", which means His presence brings light even to the darkened areas of your understanding. The opposite of light is darkness. So while He shines light on you He gives darkness to your enemies. "And be gracious to you." The opposite of graciousness can be a legal requirement or debt, which must be paid. While He is gracious to you He keeps your enemy in contempt. "The Lord lift up His countenance on you." The opposite of lifting is bringing down or of being downtrodden. While He lifts His countenance on you He brings down His fierce anger on your enemy. While He shines His light on you He keeps your enemy in darkness.

We speak face-to-face and not back-to-back, so God's face or His countenance speaks of His presence, which means that while we enjoy His presence our enemies have His back or a 'cold shoulder'. While His face gives us peace His back wars with our enemies.

His knowledge is one, but in order to understand the laws that govern our hemisphere He gave us to eat of the Tree and the 'forbidden' and He showed to us that we must make a choice. Using Nechash or Satan He gave us the power to choose, only to snap out of it altogether by that same power of choice.

We have gone down first in order to go up. Up is better than down. To have is better than to not have. To be blessed is better than to be cursed. To dwell in light is better than to dwell in darkness, just as seeing is better than being blind. Etc.

Don't you love Him for it? Yes, He always wants you to make the right choice upon learning that the first choice wasn't good. We have no enemies for we do not seek them. We are loved and choose love and then we are the standard of God's love, even the light of the world. But if the light corrupts itself by seeking out the enemy in order to destroy them, then we cease to be God's sons (Mat. 5:9) the peacemakers.

Dualism will cease when the present age ends. Already, the earth goes through tremendous climate changes and unprecedented movements of earth's tectonic plates. It is only the beginning. The Alps will grow higher and the Himalayas.

The Rocky Mountains of Colorado grew higher right in front of our eyes a couple of decades ago. TV reporters flew over the Rockies filming this act of earth's creative movements. New Islands pop out of the sea. Earthquakes will be more frequent. California will not break away from the US mainland; I think that it will slam into the mainland. The Sierra Mountains will rise higher.

God's children must hear God's voice and move according to His navigational system otherwise we perish in those cataclysmic events. His sons (spiritual and genderless expression) are called to this:

[John 8:51] Truly, truly, I say to you, if anyone keeps My word he will never see death.

We were never supposed to ever see or taste any kind of death, physical or spiritual; but do you believe Him?

If you do believe Him then you will not waste any time, but tap into His kingdom. The sooner you come out from the quagmire of the old doctrines the sooner you take a journey on the Highway of Holiness.

The right choices in life exhilarate your progress. This melancholic sentiment like, "too bad that Adam and Eve had sinned and passed down to us the original sin" leads to nowhere. Or "it is appointed for man to die and then comes the judgment." This melancholy, sadness and desperation I can smell in my nostrils. I have been in many churches of America ad yes; I smelled these entities. I also see on people in many churches a gray ash. But why do I have to embrace the melancholic, negative and depressive. Are there no other verses that glow with life?

[John 11:26] I am (Jesus) the resurrection and the life; he who believes in Me will live even if he dies, **and everyone who lives and believes in Me will never die.** Do you believe this?"

"Everyone who lives now..." Yes Lord, but you know so many have died and they were good people, even some great men and women of God."

[John 21:22-23] Jesus said to him, "If I want him to remain until I come, what is that to you? You follow Me!" Therefore this saying went out among the brethren that **that disciple would not die**; yet Jesus did not say to him that he would not die, but only, "If I want him to remain until I come, what is that to you?"

Jesus said these words so clearly and matter-of-factly so that everyone would understand Him. Upon seeing that the statement of Jesus was so clear that John made a quick attempted to camouflage the truth that hit his spirit. I think that Jesus winked at John then.

They had the truth between themselves, which was not meant to become an official church dogma.

Indeed, it's a secret walk with Jesus. Those who are born of the Spirit sin no more; and are like wind. A secret. No one knows where they come from or where do they go. It's personal, individual and not subject to any public interpretations.

I just gave you the golden nugget of the heavenly truth, but the choice is yours. The decision is yours. Let your self be inspired and let the Holy Spirit make it come to pass.

Aaron enunciated the benediction in a very special way. This tradition continued for quite some time. The secrets of the Lord God's name YHVH were closely kept within the priestly family.

YHVH is composed of the letter YUD, two letters HEI, and one letter VAV. HEI denotes graciousness; an undeserved favor God bestows on anyone He wishes to bestow. The letter HEI appears twice in God's holy name.

The greater or more grace, as James said (4:6), speaks of the grace above, which falls on anyone below. There is the supernal and the lower grace. While God gives more grace to the humble; He wars with the proud. (The Greek word ANTITASSOMAI means to range oneself against as taking a strategic position.) Also Peter used the same figure of speech.

[1Peter 5:5] God is opposed to the proud, but gives grace to the humble.

One must humble the pride of life in order to create a hollow place. For this reason **YHVH** contains two letters HEI. The first one is above, as if waiting for man (represented by letter VAV) to humble himself in order to receive.

The second HEI (number 5) comes after VAV - a person that made room for God's grace. The First grace speaks of clothing or of being wrapped in God's grace even baptized or immersed. And that speaks of prosperity, security and yes, love. Like a baby wrapped in soft blanket. The second HEI flows like the precious ointment into the hollow place one has prepared. And that's where it wants to reside.

The letter YUD speaks of divinity (number 10). Two letters HEI mean 5+5=10, plus the Letter YUD, (number 10). 10+10=20. Number 20 speaks of divine justice. VAV (number 6) speaks of anything physical, but most of all it speaks of the physical Adam from Adamah (earth), therefore us. We see that God's holy Name encloses humanity, because the spiritual realm needs no graciousness. Only the physical realm needs sustenance, supplies, healing and restoration. The Name's number is 26. But it goes far beyond the basics.

[Exodus 22:25-27] If you lend money to My people, to the poor among you, you are not to act as a creditor to him; you shall not charge him interest. If you ever take your neighbor's cloak as a pledge, you are to return it to him before the sunset, for that is his only covering; it is his cloak for his body. What else shall he sleep in? And it shall come about that when he cries out to Me, I will hear him, **for I am gracious.**

I will certainly hear Him because I am gracious. Anything wrong touches God's extremely sensitive heart. Learn it now before you go any further.

We are being sandwiched between Divinity (YUD) and His double graciousness. However, our cooperation in this process is greatly required; otherwise the above is just a head-knowledge. Trying to impress someone with knowledge or even wisdom is not the goal here.

Israel surrounded by their enemies when Aaron spoke the benediction over the people and in such situation every single word had a much deeper meaning. Automatically the dread of the God of Abraham Isaac and Jacob fell on Israel's enemies when the name of God was uttered.

While the angel of death passed through the households of the Egyptians, no harm had befallen the Israelite households. While God was showing His love toward the people of Israel, He fought the Egyptians; later on the Amalekites; and then the Canaanites. His face was turned toward Israel, but His back was turned toward Israel's enemies.

Some ridiculous teaching goes around postulating that as it was with the Egyptians who did not smear the blood of the lamb on their doors; and their firstborns died; we Christians should plead the blood of Jesus and apply it daily on our lives. As a result people keep on doing it as a daily ritual. They fear the onslaught of the devil and kept on pleading the blood of Jesus as if trembling in fear just in case the enemy would do what it did to the Egyptians.

In their eyes the enemy was made so great that it obscured the power of the Almighty God. Those mediocre teachings stem only from tremendous insecurity, which is then fueled by fear, which in turn are fueled by ignorance.

Why people are so quick embracing stupidity and are so slow to embrace wisdom; still makes me wonder. Why those good meaning Christians identify themselves with the Egyptians rather than with Israel? Perhaps they have nothing to do with the chosen people of God?

What is happening today in the Middle East is frightful. ISIS is slaughtering Christians and ethnic minorities as well the Shia Muslims whom they label heretics. Since the world became secular, USA and Europe do but little to eradicate this evil. But all these Middle Eastern Christians have nothing to do with the Jew or Israel. They have been kept in blindness. All they know is the church, incense, golden crosses, figures, pictures, crossings, rosaries and Eucharist or Mass; that's all. Christian America will not fight for them nor will Israel, and much less the united Europe. So what's going on? Where is the God of Abraham, Isaac and Israel? He is totally forgotten in confines of the man-made religion. But His word is alive and all His promises come to pass.

During this period of great turmoil there will be a voice crying to unite all Arabs against Israel to destroy it and that will be the day when multitudes will swarm the plains of Megiddo.

God will then make it personal. The carnage will be most incredible and the world will watch and say that there is no other God, but the God of Israel.

ISIS will grow in strength even some from the Syrian and Iraqi army will defect and join ISIS. They expect their messiah too and this army of young men exploits this sentiment with words like Caliphate, Islamic State, etc. It's a ploy only to gather men from all nations. When their numbers swell they will becomes the leaders of Islam and then they will unite their front against Israel.

Israel smeared the lamb's blood in obedience to God's word and not out of fear. Yes, Moses told them what God told him, and Aaron transmitted it to the people. It was their blind obedience to God's word; for how can anyone imagine an angel of death, or death of thousands, in a single night. It was just too incredible. They backed up their faith with a work. The end-result was that they were not afraid, for like Peter (NT) they also walked on water. Peter (Gospels) walked on the word of Jesus, which was the simple word "come." The Israelites did the same by obeying God's word. Had they looked around like Peter did, they would have sunk into the scary sea of fear.

I know what I've got. I have the living and the best spiritual food in the entire world. I know who I am and I am very secure in His word, that is the reason I may sound like I am tooting my own horn. If I may come across as being proud, then know this, this is the truth even the sharp and cutting two-edged sword. If you do not like this cutting and want me to prance around your humanistic sensitivities and beat around the bush then I have no business of writing anything and call it the truth. Facts are facts. One cannot change them.
"Sorry" for letting you know what I know. Humanism was developed for those whose bodies are so important that everyone should respect them, even God who created them.
We must realize that for God all flesh is as grass (Isaiah 40:7-8) and it has little meaning, except for the ones called His seed. He has huge 'factories of genetics.' Today, we can clone our bodies. But can we clone His NESHAMAH?
Either you stay humanistic or you become godly. If I have not sparked any interest in the divine things in you then I have failed, but if I have reached at least one, I've reached the world.

* * *

Chapter 19

WHEN I REPENTED

Before we part let me lead you along that path of repentance and its glorious experience.

Once you open that door you will let in the essence of God's love. Like most precious perfume it will permeate the atmosphere.

When I made the decision to wholeheartedly repent; I went up to my room, and got on my knees.

Some strange feeling came over me, so powerful that it made me run downstairs... but to do what? I did not have a clue. I was scatterbrained and thought I'm losing it, for I started to walk around the coffee table like a chicken with its head cut off. I ran to the refrigerator, but could not find in it anything satisfying. That's when I realized that these are not demons, or the devil, but the 'old Adam' laden with ancestral baggage. Upon realizing it I tapped into the free agency of my will, which I did not use too often. Subconsciously I knew that I have the power to do it. I went upstairs and got on my knees. Then the same feeling almost lifted me off my knees and I did the same as before. I walked nervously around the coffee table. Was I crazy? What was going on?

Finally, I went upstairs for the third time, but this time with a much greater determination. This time my resolve was complete. I remained on my knees and shut the 'old Adam' up by saying, "I love my Father more. I love my Creator more. I love my Savior more than anything else or any other feeling."

I knew that I had to do it in order to overrule the flesh. I expressed my commitment and my love for my Master.

Amazingly, words were sort of given to me to say, which the 'I', the self-identity, the ego, did not want to say. I was really divided.

The natural and divine were being separated. The sword of which we read in God's Word had then been applied.

[Hebrews 4:12] For the word of God is living, active, and sharper than any two-edged sword, and piercing as far as the division of soul and spirit.

God, the Spirit, showed me what was in my ancestral line; who did what, and all its awful hideous, loathsome things, which had provoked God to anger.

Yes, the wrath of God was upon a branch of my family for some, like Cain, have turned their back to Him.

I saw what they have done and how they have grieved Him. I was then expected to do something about it. Upon realizing it I quickly apologized and asked God to have mercy on that branch of my ancestry. I did it with tears. Being as in a trance, I could see more and more, as I was able to look beyond time.

Each time I saw a hand, picking up something awful, dangling it in front of me. I saw something like a dead shriveled up and awfully smelling frog. At the same time He showed me what each picture meant. Instantly I knew what it was and cried for mercy.

"What shall I do with this?" was the question.

"I hate it! Destroy it! I love you more!" I cried to God in tears.

I was shown many hidden things and each time I was asked to deal with these things. None of these things were just removed, but He kept asking me what He ought do with them; as if testing me to the very end, who or as to what I love more.

This was amazing; He respects our choices so much that although I did not commit or adopt the things that were in my ancestry tree, still it pleased God and I felt it. I was merciful not just to myself; I interceded for those who were before me in my family tree.

Although I cannot help the dead, but definitely, through it, I was helping myself - the now living. Nonetheless, I knew that I was made responsible for my ancestors for I acted on the passed-down-to-me impulses. I have walked in their shoes.

I chose not only to not walk in my ancestors' shoes, but I did more. I cleansed even them and my family tree. God gave me the knowledge that the entire family tree was cleansed. In God there is no time, what I do and what my predecessors did is one timeless unit before the all-knowing One.

During the entire repentance process the air smelled as if someone opened a sewer and I could hardly breathe, it was so intense.

When He showed me the last image—filled with meaning and history as to how it all came to be in the first place—upon seeing it I was torn to the core of my being and sincerely apologized to God. At that point I was free and elated.

Peace and tremendous joy enveloped my being; a feeling I never knew. The air changed. Instead of the fetid sewage-like smell, this time it was filled with sweet heavenly perfume.

Today I am quite sure that I had then extracted the love essence I was so long longing for. I was filled with light and was flying. I've been flying ever since.

I am being loved and now by sharing it with you, you are being loved. It's a good thing to be made out of wax. Like a candle we come closer to Him. So let the hot flame of His love melt you and absorb you into its realm. You are in His holy presence. Be a candle too.

www.ingramcontent.com/pod-product-compliance
Lightning Source LLC
Chambersburg PA
CBHW070649050426
42451CB00008B/326